THE COMPLEXITIES OF ACCULTURATION AND ORTHOGONAL CULTURAL IDENTIFICATION IN RICHARD FLANAGAN'S FICTION

DR. ANISHA SINDHU

Contents

Preface

Richard Flanagan is a well known Australian writer who bagged Man Booker Prize in 2014 for his exceptional novel *The Narrow Road to the Deep North*. I, as a research scholar, got an opportunity to explore the writings of this legend from the cultural perspective. After I successfully defended my Ph.D. thesis, the pannel members including the external examiner strongly recommended that this research work deserves to take the form of a book and reach to the people. The simple reason for this is that the study tends to explore the psychological implications of cultural interaction on an individual or a group of individuals who come in contact with two or more different cultures and how the whole society is affected by the cultural changes.

I really hope, as is also intended, that this book helps the readers to understand all the possible effects of cultural interaction and the subsequent changes on the people and the society, hence giving better insight into the possible solutions to cope up with these changes.

Acknowledgements

In the first place, praises and thanks to the Almighty, for His showers of blessings throughout my research work to complete the research successfully.

I would like to express my deep and sincere gratitude to my research supervisor, Dr. Balkar Singh, Associate Professor, Lovely Professional University, Phagwara for giving me the opportunity to do research and provide valuable guidance and constant support throughout this research.

I express my thankfulness to Prof. Rabinder Powar, Punjabi University, Patiala; Dr. Pavitar Parkash Singh, Head of School, LPU; Dr. Ajoy Batta, Head of the Department of English, LPU; and Dr. Rekha, Assistant Dean, Centre for Research Degree Programmes, LPU, Phagwara, Dr. Digvijay Pandya, Dr. Sanjay Prasad Panday and Dr. Gowher Naik for their support throughout this research work. I am extendingmy thanks to all the panelists of annual seminars for their constant feedback and kindness. I want to grab this opportunity to thank the panel members Dr. Digvijay Pandya, Dr. Sanjay Prasad Panday, and Dr. Gowher Naik.

I am extremely grateful to my parents Dr. Maha Singh Sindhu and Mrs Saroj Sindhu, uncle Mr. Ramkishan Sindhu and Aunt Mrs. Nirmal Malik for their love, prayers, and sacrifices for educating and preparing me for my future. My father, Dr. Maha Singh Sindhu has bben a source of motivation and has always been giving a push to finish the research work quickly. My special thanks to my friend Dr. Shikha Thakur, my brother Nishant Sindhu and my cousin Mansha Malik for their continuous encouragement to make me complete this work successfully.

Finally, my acknowledgements to all the people who have supported me complete this research work directly or indirectly. Without their support and the constant motivation, especially by my father, this research wouldn't have been possible.

Introduction

In today's world, along with the high-tech developments and globalization, it is challenging for cultures to remain isolated and uninfluenced by other cultures. However, no one knows how many people have left their own culture to make that one dominant culture more dominating. There is no count of the total number of cultures being practiced all over the world. Nevertheless, when an individual or a group of people comes in contact with a new culture, there arises a state of internal chaos as to whether to maintain one's culture or merge in the new culture altogether. The person who interacts with the dominant culture begins having internal chaos. Will the people of the dominant culture accept the person from the non-dominant culture? Will the society of the non-dominant culture let the person choose the dominant culture and leave his own culture behind?

Some sociologists, psychologists, and anthropologists have tried and explained the process of mixing two cultures. They have even tried to sum up the psychological state of the person who has to change. Usually, the person or group who has to change is who immigrates into a new society. The most important question that arises here is- What is culture?

According to Georg Simmel, a sociologist, culture is "the cultivation of individuals through the agency of external forms which have been objectified in the course of history." Merriam Webster Dictionary has defined culture as:

1. "the customary beliefs, social forms, and material traits of a racial, religious, or social group"
2. "the set of shared attitudes, values, goals, and practices that characterizes an institution or organization"
3. "the set of values, conventions, or social practices associated with a particular field, activity, or societal characteristic"

4. "the integrated pattern of human knowledge, belief, and behavior that depends upon the capacity for learning and transmitting knowledge to succeeding generations"

Acculturation is the process in which the migrants move to a new culture and develop relationships with it and maintain their original culture (Berry & Sam 42). According to Berry and Sam in 1997 stated that acculturation involves four strategies: assimilation, separation, integration, and marginalization.

Acculturation is when one culture, typically the dominant one, transfers its traits to another culture, a less dominant or the non-dominant one. There has been much discussion on this topic of acculturation. Various eminent scholars from different fields, like psychology, sociology, anthropology, human geography, geography, etc., have defined acculturation according to various perspectives. For example, according to Fred Beauvais, if there is a straight line and on the left end, there is the non-dominant culture, whereas on the right end, there is the dominant culture, and if a person wants to move from left to right, that is, from non-dominant towards the dominant culture, he will keep on loosing traits of his own culture and will face the inner as well as the outer conflict, this is acculturation.

According to Merriam Webster Dictionary, acculturation is

1. "cultural modification of an individual, group, or people by adapting to or borrowing traits from another culture.
2. the process by which a human being acquires the culture of a particular society from infancy."

Stating the difference between Enculturation and Acculturation, Berry and others, in 1992, have said that "the former is the process that links developing individuals to their primary cultural contexts, while the latter is a process that individuals undergo in response to a changing cultural context" (62). Further, they have also stated that it is challenging to separate the changes that are caused due to external factors from those that are caused due to internal factors, which occur when two cultures come in contact. A person or a group of people get influenced by the dominant culture.

In the book entitled *Anthropology: Race, Language, Culture, Psychology, Prehistory* the anthropologist Kroeber, in 1948, stated that

> *"... acculturation comprises those changes in one culture brought about by contact with another culture, resulting in an increased similarity between the two cultures. This type of change, according may be reciprocal, however, very often the process is asymmetrical and the result is the (usually partial) absorption of one culture into the other. (19)"*

The first definition of acculturation was given by Redfield, Linton, and Herskovits in 1936: "Acculturation comprehends those phenomena which result when groups of individuals having different cultures come into continuous first-hand contact, with subsequent changes in the original culture patterns of either or both groups" (149). The term acculturation is often confused with Assimilation, Enculturation, Cultural Diffusion, Cultural Appropriation, and Amalgamation. According to Berry in 1974, assimilation is one of the sectors chosen by the person who acculturates. According to his four-fold model of acculturation, assimilation occurs when a person has very little interest in maintaining his own culture. At the same time, he seeks to adapt to the new culture, whereas, in acculturation, a person can choose to maintain his culture or leave his culture. The term *enculturation* refers to the acquiring values and norms through unconscious repetition, which is usually by birth. In other words, it is a process when an individual or a group of individuals gets more involved in their own culture. In comparison, acculturation occurs when one adopts the traits from another culture. The following term that is closely related to acculturation is *cultural diffusion*. Both the terms are used in Anthropology with a notable difference. Cultural diffusion occurs when the traits of one culture spread to another culture. In contrast, acculturation occurs when an individual or a group of individuals transform by adopting the traits of the dominant culture as a result of cultural contact. In short, Cultural diffusion assists acculturation. Cultural appropriation is a very negative term used to describe a process when the traits of a culture, usually the less dominant or the non-dominant, are mocked by the people of the dominant culture. Amalgamation is the blending of two or more cultures, whereas acculturation is when an individual or a group eliminates one and adopts another culture.

Berry has given a four-fold model of acculturation- assimilation, segregation, integration, marginalization. According to Berry, it is a state in which the immigrants show little interest in maintaining their own culture and prefer to adopt the society's culture where they seek to settle. Segregation is a possibility when the immigrants avoid maintaining relations with their own culture and ultimately adopt or meet down in the dominant or the target culture. In his research paper published in 200, Berry stated that this term, segregation, becomes separation when applied to a larger society. This close relation is the reason that these two terms are used interchangeably. Marginalization- This condition leads to the loss of identity of the immigrant, where he rejects both cultures. This process is the most negative of all the other acculturation processes as the other processes have some positive implications or effects on society and the individual's psyche. Integration- This is the most common way the immigrants choose to keep both the cultures, which means cultural maintenance and involvement with the larger society are sought. It has been observed that this is the most commonly seen process of acculturation that leaves positive effects on both the psyche of the individual and society as a whole. The figure below was given by Berry, clearly stating the base and the principle of the four-fold model of acculturation.

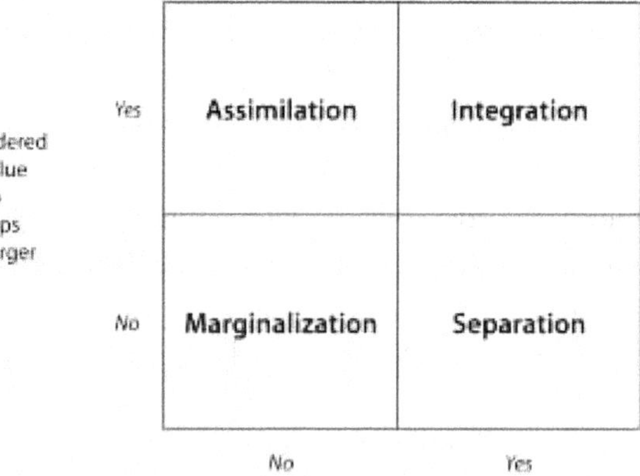

Figure1: Berry J.W.

John Widdup Berry (J.W. Berry) is a psychologist by profession. People know him because of his extraordinary work mainly in two fields: ecological and cultural influences on behavior; and the adaptation of immigrants and indigenous peoples following intercultural contact. He has researched mainly in Cross-Cultural Psychology and has developed two concepts; one is acculturative stress. The other is the acculturation strategies which are also known as the processes of acculturation. Acculturative stress, according to Berry, is the psychological pressure that the immigrants undergo when they come in contact with a new culture- "a negative psychological reaction to the experiences of acculturation, often characterized by anxiety, depression, and a variety of psychosomatic problems" (475). Acculturation strategy, according to Berry and others, is- "the way that individuals and ethnocultural groups orient themselves to the process of acculturation. Four strategies are: assimilation, integration, separation, and marginalization" (475).

Berry has been researching acculturation since 1974 and has recently published one more research paper in the same line. He is considered a prominent theorist as his model is one of the strong pillars in acculturation theory. It would not be wrong to state that the research is done in the field of acculturation after Berry propagated his four-fold model of acculturation. He has received many awards for being an extraordinary researcher and has published more than one hundred and twenty articles in various journals and two hundred book chapters. He has over one lakh citations and has an h-index of 110 on Google Scholar. There are various theories on acculturation given by various scholars. Hieu Van Ngo has discussed the phases of acculturation in his research paper titled 'A critical examination of acculturation theories'- Unidirectional, Bidimensional, and Interactive acculturation. JW Berry has given a four-fold model talking about the involvement of two cultures and the possibilities an immigrant can go through while interacting with other cultures.

Orthogonal cultural identification theory came out in 1991 and is based on a principle which states that in a society which has pluralistic nature, an individual is free to identify with more than one culture without letting the identification with other cultures be affected. The main idea of this theory is that association with any one culture has no relation with belongingness to other cultures. Cultural identification is an ever-changing process that has always been debatable and questioned for a particular definition. However, it can be defined as following a lifestyle of a particular culture (e.g., living day-to-day life with the people who belong to the same culture, participating and celebrating the tradition and the rituals, food habits, dressing style, behavior in a particular situation, etc.). A simple example of the complex nature of cultural identity is that the people who belong to one culture may or may not have an inclination towards belongingness with one or more other cultures or even no association with any culture at the same time as every individual is different, and so are their choices. Cultural identification is very different from the ethnic identity which Oetting and Beauvais, the proponents of the theory, in their 1991 research paper mentioned. They stated that before knowing what cultural identity is, it is essential to know what it is not. Cultural identity is an umbrella term that has an ethnic identity as a part of it.

This theory is said to have made a vital contribution in the development of the fields of research and counseling, as it has completely normalized the multicultural identification experiences of an individual and also considered a pluralistic society as an ideal society for the growth of an individual as well as the society as a whole. All the previously established theories of acculturation had a fundamental principle: there is always a loss of identification with the culture of origin while adopting the dominant cultural identity. This theory is critical because it draws one step further from all the previously established acculturation theories by normalizing the multicultural identification and proving that there is no change in the degree of identification with one culture with the increase or decrease in the degree of identification with any other culture or more than one culture. Moreover, the orthogonal cultural identification scale that comes with this theory provides a quantitative method to measure the degrees of identification of an individual with one or more cultures and provides that accuracy in unfolding the complex nature of cultural identification. The scale gives a range of four options to answer from, for measuring her/his cultural identification with one or more cultures, asking to answer eight questions taking a deep dive into the very core of this complex process. It proves that an individual may change the degree of identification with one culture without affecting the degree of identification with another culture.

Richard Flanagan was born in 1961 in Longford, Tasmania, Australia. The Economist considers him to be one of the finest Australian novelists of his generation. He won the Man Booker Prize for his novel *The Narrow*

Road to the Deep North in 2014. It is said that when the Great Famine hit Ireland, his family was transported to Australia, and this is also a known fact about Richard Flanagan that he has the Irish convicts as his forefathers. His father was a Burma Death Railway survivor, which becomes the semi-autobiographical element in his Booker Prize- winning novel *The Narrow Road to the Deep North.* Till six years of age, he suffered a severe hearing disease that followed him since his birth. Flanagan had a few personal issues. He had to leave the schooling at the age of sixteen. However, he was able to resume his studies at the University of Tasmania. In 1983, he became the president of a union known as the Tasmania University Union. He graduated with a Bachelor of Arts with a First-Class Honors degree. He received Lifetime Achievement Award in 2005, awarded by International Academy for Intercultural Research. Flanagan published four works of non-fiction before he started writing fiction, works he has called "his apprenticeship." He has written seven non-fiction works of great importance. They are- *A Terrible Beauty: History of the Gordon River Country* (1985), *The Rest of the World Is Watching — Tasmania and the Greens* (1990), *Codename Iago: The Story of John Friedrich* (1991), *Parish-Fed Bastards. A History of the Politics of the Unemployed in Britain, 1884–1939* (1991), *And What Do You Do, Mr. Gable?* (2011), *Notes On An Exodus* (2015), *Seize the Fire: Three speeches* (2018). Apart from non-fiction works, Flanagan has proved his worth in fiction also. He has written seven pretty fascinating novels. His first novel, *Death of a River Guide*, was published in 1994. After the success of this book, there were six more books in a row to win the hearts of the fiction lovers. His second book, *The Sound of One Hand Clapping* came out in 1997, *Gould's Book of Fish: A Novel in Twelve Fish* in 2001, *The Unknown Terrorist* in 2006, *Wanting* in 2008, *The Narrow Road to the Deep North* 2013, and his latest novel *First Person* was published in 2017. Flanagan has also tried his hand at writing film scripts. He was the director and the scriptwriter of 'The Sound of One Hand Clapping' (1998). It is a drama film based on the novel of the same name. In 2008, he co-wrote an epic romantic historical drama film 'Australia.'

Richard Flanagan's *Death of a River Guide* is a novel which has a description of three generations, narrated by the protagonist Aljaz Cosini, who is drowning in the river and has been granted visions in which he can see the life of his father, grandfather and many other people who died before his birth. Aljaz comes to know about the history of Tasmania in his visions as he sees the history of the members of his family. The plot of the novel is a complex one as he narrates the stories at three different levels. Aljaz is made to believe that they immigrated to Australia with their own will, but through the visions, it becomes clear that they have a convict ancestry and have not descended from a white man. A convict named Ned Quade used to be who escaped the prison and looked out for shelter here in Tasmania. This vision fills Aljaz with a sense of more belongingness to the land than he ever felt before. With the history of his ancestry, Aljaz also envisions the history of Tasmania till the present day. It shocks Aljaz that the fact the histories have told that is wrong. The books of history tell us that all the black aborigines were either shifters or murdered and that there are no black aborigines in Tasmania anymore. However, the fact is that they still exist. The love life of Aljaz is not peaceful at all. He is in love with a girl named Couta Ho, with whom he also has a daughter. The drowning Aljaz envisions their lives. They are delighted as Couta gives birth to a baby girl, but their life changes completely after their infant daughter dies. Couta holds Aljaz to be responsible for it and cannot overcome the grief of the loss. There comes a gap between the two. Couta starts believing that her husband does not understand her and can never really feel the pain and grief she is going through because she is the one who bore the girl inside her for nine months. She has all the attachment to her as she is the one who stayed with Jemma day and night and not Aljaz, who was always out for work.

The river trip that proves to be the last trip for Aljaz begins when his boss forces Aljaz to go on the expedition, being an experienced guide. He meets a fascinating character here named Cockroach, who is a co-guide with him. There comes the point where Aljaz drowns in the water and keeps on going down. Aljaz realizes that his life and the life of other members of his family start moving in from his eyes. And then he realizes that he is not dying despite being drowned for so long because he has been granted visions. Through the visions, Aljaz sees the life he has already lived and the lives of his father and grandfather, and even the first ancestor of his family. He also envisions the actual history of Tasmania that the history creators hid.

The Sound of One Hand Clapping revolves around Sonja, a three-year-old protagonist at the beginning of the novel, whose parents have shifted from Slovenia to Australia in search of better food, a better job, in short, a better lifestyle. Since the beginning of the novel, the readers are informed that Sonja's mother and her father are uncomfortable with the new environment but are forced to adjust to dominant Australian society. The politician of the area indirectly pressurizes the immigrants or the people of minority culture to forget their shameful and poor life and adopt the ways of Australia. If they want to be happy and earn money, they need to do as per the sayings of the politician. It is not only the politician who forces or pressurizes them; instead, he is the voice of all the people of the dominant culture. The poor immigrants have no choice but to agree with the people of the dominant culture. Maria leaves the town leaving behind her three-year-old daughter Sonja and her husband, Bojan. This novel runs back and forth in time. Even the names of the chapters are the years of the incidents described in the chapter. The novel started in 1954 when Sonja was three years old to when she turned sixteen in 1967. Then the story jumps to the year 1989 when Sonja turns thirty-eight years old. Now when Sonja is a grown-up older woman, we know that she has left her father back in Tasmania and shifts to the elite area of Australia, Sydney. She visits her father, and on her way back home, she is surrounded by all the memories still alive somewhere in her brain. Mostly, she remembers the bad memories associated with Tasmania.

Gould's Book of Fish is a masterpiece in itself. The book is written in twelve chapters printed in different colors, where each color signifies something. This novel is based on the real-life experience of a convict in Australia. William Buelow Gould is the protagonist of the novel, and he is also an unreliable narrator who alternates the narration with Sid Hammet. This novel has very little to do with the storyline and the characters. Instead, Gould's protagonist travels different places and most of the novel is about his thought process. Sid Hammet is the one who finds Gould's version of the book of fish. He reads it, and when he plans to research it and tell people about the actual history of the penal colony, he forgets it on the counter of a pub. He has no proof of what he read. He stares at a fish. Now, this fish has become very important. The second part of the story revolves around the actual experiences of Gould. It is tough to trace the background of Gould for two reasons; one, he does not know who he is, and second, he denies what he has said before and hence is a very unreliable person.

In America, Gould meets a man named Jean-Babeuf Audubon, who is an artist. Gould never wanted to be a painter, but somehow he learns it and starts using the identity of a painter whenever he falls in a troublesome situation. First, Gould uses an artist's identity faking to be a painter, but then he realizes that he is an artist and starts painting from his heart and soul. Gould is hired by many people who are not happy with his work, and this way, finally, he lands up in prison, where the prison doctor hires him.

Gould, one day, gets a chance to swim in the flooded prison and reach the recorded cell of the prison. He realizes that the history is written for the world to read about the penal colony does not tell the actual brutal nature of the officers and the sufferings of the prisoners who are arrested without any crime. Instead, history glorifies the rulers' success and how effectively they rule the colony and control the criminals. He finally succeeds in escaping the prison and hides in the interiors of Tasmania, where something magical happens, and Gould realizes that he has now become a fish. Now, Gould, in the form of a fish, is the same fish that Sid Hammet is staring at.

Gould falls in love with a black aborigine on the island whose name is Twopenny Sal. Although she has a small role to play and nothing to contribute in the story of fish by Gould, she turns out to be a significant character from the perspective of the superiority and inferiority of cultures and the power and brutality of the dominant culture and the helplessness and the sufferings of the people who belong to the minority culture. Twopenny Sal catches the eyes of some white men who decide to take her to their country as a full-time slave. When they come to know that she will never agree to go with them, they kidnap her son and condition that they return her son only because she accompanies them. She finds herself very helpless and agrees to their condition, having no choice to say no. The moment she lands in the area dominated by the whites and from where she could never return to her land on her own, the white masters kill her son by smashing his head on a rock. She gets pregnant with her masters many times but takes her revenge by killing her children which she gave birth to by the white masters. She becomes a perfect example of a black aborigine woman who, when decided, can do anything even in a foreign land where she has no one whom she can call hers.

Wanting is like an expensive cloth woven with many colorful threads representing the people and events taken from history, one of which he also weaved in his previous novel that is Gould's Book of Fish. Similarly, in *Wanting*, Towterer, aka King Romeo, is the chieftain of a Tasmanian tribe. This beautiful novel tells the story of the effects of two or more cultures mixing up. There is a little black aborigine girl named Mathinna, whose other name is Leda. She is christened with the name of Leda by the Protector, who is assigned the task of civilizing the black aborigines by the ruling and the dominant people of white culture. For this purpose, the Protector makes a colony of some houses built up in the way of the whites and teaches the black aborigines the lifestyle of the whites. For example, the black aborigines are given food eaten by the whites to get habitual to it. Towterer is the father of Mathinna but lives away from her as the Protector takes her, and Towterer could not keep him from taking his daughter away. The author has filled almost all the characters with a 'wanting' desire that burns in them. However, Mathinna, Lady Jane, and Towterer are amongst the leading ones.

The Unknown Terrorist is another beautiful novel by Richard Flanagan, which has a story of a dark girl Ginna, who is known as Doll, throughout the novel. She has a low-income family background, and this is why earning money becomes her only goal in life. She moves to Sydney, Australia, and starts working as a prostitute with the same purpose in life. She does not consider this profession wrong, but she finds it difficult to sleep with different persons every night. She is very fond of brands. She dreams of buying a branded handbag and tells her friend that she has saved money for this Louis Vuitton handbag. One day, when she and her best friend Wilder go to a beach for the latter's son to have an ideal space to play, the former meets a tall, dark, and handsome man named Tariq. Tariq saves the life of Wilder's son, and from that moment on, the Doll feels attracted to that man. Soon the two develop a romantic relationship. They make out in his apartment, but in the morning, Doll finds a note that said "Had to fly. Call you soon." (85) After some days, the Doll finds out that Tariq is a terrorist and that the cops of the town are in a search for him. Just because of that one night, the Doll gets in trouble as she is seen with Tariq in the CCTV cameras. The unknown terrorist of the novel is her lover, who may or may not be an Al Qaeda operator planting bombs around the city.

The Narrow Road to the Deep North is a booker prize-winning novel with many layers of stories running parallel. The protagonist of the novel is Dorrigo Evans is an Australian aborigine. He is a well-educated man who serves as a doctor in the Japanese POW camp. The story takes an exciting turn when Dorrigo indulges in a two-sided love affair with his uncle's young wife. He gets many chances to make this relation more and more intimate. Richard Flanagan's life's many incidents are depicted in this novel, and hence the novel is semi-autobiographical. Apart from his love life with his aunt, he has a loving wife who never doubts her husband. However, Dorrigo does not feel the same way with his aunt Amy as he finds himself addicted to the curves and fragrance of the latter's body. This aspect is one side of the novel.

The second side of the novel is ruthless. The Japanese government attacks the weaker countries, takes the people of the defeated countries as prisoners of war and makes them work as slaves day and night, starving for food and living in very unhygienic conditions. There are people from different countries who live together under one roof and have good relations. However, some people carry hatred and prejudice in their hearts for the people they live with and belong to the countries they hate. As a result, people die of hunger and diseases that are very painful and awful to look at. Dorrigo tries his best to save as many people as he can but sometimes finds himself helpless. The role of the supremacy of the dominant culture is very vital in giving shape to the novel. The Japanese are dominant and powerful in most of the novel. They treat other people as sheer waste and as non-humans. For instance, they can beat up an individual in the middle of so many people gathered around. However, the people, who want to come forward and help, find themselves helpless as the beaters belong to the dominant and influential culture.

Similarly, in the latter half of the novel, when Japan gets out of power and America becomes the ruling country, the same Japanese who used to practice their power are now forced to be quiet and mum and behave according to the rules and regulations of the now powerful America. However, some characters like Major Nakamura are and have always been proud of being from Japan. Even after the downfall of the Japanese government, when he shifts to America to live a more peaceful life, he says when asked that he is Japanese and is proud to be, with the fact known that being Japanese is not quite acceptable because of the tortures that Japanese did in their golden period. Nevertheless, some characters change their identity wherever they go and whatever is the demand of the situation.

Acculturation and Orthogonal Cultural Identification theory have psychological and social implications also. Berry's acculturation model provides us with four alternatives out of which an immigrant or an individual from a minority culture can opt for one. Every sub-category of the four processes has different social and psychological impacts. It has been observed that when a decision to assimilate, segregate, integrate or marginalize is forced on an individual or a group of people that belongs to a minority culture, then the effect on the psyche of the individual and the society as a whole is negative. There arises a lot of chaos and disturbance in the society in the form of riots etc. that costs the lives of many people belonging to the majority and minority cultures. It has been observed in the studies by the research scholars that generally, marginalization has very adverse effects on an individual's psyche that goes to the extent of even suicide. The integration process is the most positive out of four, even when forced by the dominant culture people on the non- dominant one. The negative impact does not harm someone's psyche, forcing her/him to go into a state of depression. However, the perfect state or the ideal state is that of orthogonal cultural identification. In this condition, the individual can practice as many cultures as possible without affecting the degree of association with other cultures. In such a state, the individual's psyche and society are at peace as there is no internal or external pressure on members of any dominant or non-dominant cultures.

Acculturation is the new normal these days because of the processes like globalization. People from various cultures interact with each other for several reasons. First, the structure of society is rapidly changing. Second, people's tolerance for their peaceful co-existence with the people of other cultures has increased with time. All the countries in the world are multicultural these days as the people from different cultures migrate to a new culture, and the majority of them choose to integrate. This willing acceptance of the integration process makes the people around, the psyche of the individual and society, work very peacefully and grows to new heights. Nevertheless, the people who migrate have different opinions and thought processes, and due to this, all of them have a different take on the choice of acculturation. For example, some people may not find it ethical to forget their culture of origin. For someone, leaving one's own culture behind and assimilating in the dominant culture is a piece of cake and the only correct option, and they do it willingly. Nevertheless, sometimes, the choice to choose is not made by the migrants or the people of minority culture but is the demand of the dominant culture. As a result, they force the people of non-dominant cultures with the help of government policies or by the use of police force. This process negatively affects the psyche of the individual as well as the society as a whole.

Richard Flanagan, as a writer, has portrayed characters which belong to every category of the cultures of society. Out of these characters, some choose to assimilate by their own will and hence fall under the category of 'melting pot,' which depicts a significant portion of the society these days migrating to the developed cultures. Ziggy Heidl, a significant character in the novel *First Person*, is born in South Australia but moves to Germany when he turns 26. He adopts the German accent, forgetting the accent of his mother tongue that he used for the first 26 years of his life (5), which is his own decision. Similarly, Bojan Buloh, the father of the protagonist of *The Sound of One Hand Clapping*, owns a car that he names 'FJ' in Australia and once says to his daughter, "... it was a proof to both those in Slovenia and Australia that he had become what he had set out to be: Australian." (85) This quote shows how Bojan willingly assimilates into the Australian culture, which he is proud to do, and leaves Slovenian one. The best example of *a* 'melting pot' is Mathinna, a black aborigine protagonist of *Wanting*. She desires to be like the elite white people, and when she gets a chance to be like one of them, she gives her best and learns about their lifestyle. There are various other characters in all his novels that represent this sect of immigrants.

The following sect of the migrants is of those who either choose or are forced to choose to follow the process of segregation. Flanagan has very beautifully portrayed the character's psyche and the effect of this process on society as a whole. For instance, Robinson, a character in *Wanting*, who is given a task by the white people who belong to the dominant culture and he is supposed to civilize the black aborigines and make them behave in the way the latter do, notes that

> *"... the more they died, the more they wanted to cast off their English clothes and stop eating their English food, and move out of their English homes, which they said were filled with the Devil, and return to the pleasures of the hunt of a day and the open fire of a night. (2)"*

The people of Australia segregate themselves from all the lures of being a part of the dominant culture. Flanagan depicts many other characters which fall into this category. These days, the third type of migrants who integrate with the dominant culture either by their wish or force. Nevertheless, in both cases, the lives of the people, their psyche, and the society around them have a very positive impact. All of Flanagan's novels are loaded with characters that represent this sect of society. For example, when Mathinna, the protagonist of *Wanting*, lies alone in her expensive bed, she tries to unravel her many fathers. "... God her Father, and Jesus his Son, who was also a sort of a father; there was the Protector, who had the Spirit of God the Father; and then there was Sir John, who was also her father, her new father— so many fathers." (113) However, she writes the letter to her father that is Towterer. This introspection of Mathinna shows that she considers the people of the majority culture to be her father, the God and His Son as her fathers, and of course, her father, Towterer. However, the chronology, with which she recalls all her fathers, shows that she has very well integrated with the English society. According to Berry, then there is one more sect of migrants, which is those who either choose or are forced to marginalize that is not to associate or belong to any of the cultures. Flanagan's novels have representation of this sect of people as well. It has been observed that this process has the most harmful effects on the characters' psyche, which represents the people who migrate and society as a whole. Choi Sang-min is a Korean character in *The Narrow Road to the Deep North*, brought up in a Japanese-ruled country. In his childhood, he was forced to be alienated as he, being a Korean, is not accepted by the Japanese and is punished by the Japanese for speaking in his native language that is Korean. As he grows up, he decides to leave both cultures voluntarily when he realizes that if he says that he belongs to the dominant country, he will get fifty yen, "I am not Korean, he thought to himself. I am not Japanese. I am a man of a colony. Where is my fifty yen? He wanted to know. Where? " (347). He realizes that he has no particular identity as he has been named differently by people of different cultures. This loss of identity is a result of the uncertainty of belongingness with any one culture. Initially, it was forced by the dominant and ruling Japanese people, and then the withdrawal was voluntary. Similarly, Bojan Buloh, a character in *The Sound of One Hand Clapping*, lies in an abyss as he feels as if he belongs nowhere. Initially, he proudly leaves the culture of origin but later feels that he has not been accepted by the people of the dominant culture as well. He clears his thinking about their belonging to one particular culture when he replies to Sonja's wish to return home. He says, "Where? What home? You and I have no home. Don't you understand? ... We have a wog flat, my Sonja. A wog flat. Don't you understand? ..." (374)

Flanagan has not only painted the characters which face the chaos of only two cultures, but he also portrays many characters who fall under the most accepted process. This process does not belong to the bi-cultural societies but belongs to the multicultural or cultural pluralistic societies. This process is the condition of those who simultaneously use different degrees of association to various cultures. One degree of identification is not affected by the increase or decrease in the degree of identification with any other culture. This process is an ideal state of the society to live in as it has hardly any adverse effect on the psyche of the individual and the society as a whole. The majority of the population in modern times belongs to this category, and hence Flanagan has also painted many of his characters very beautifully, representing this sect of the migrants. For example, Bojan, a character of *The Sound of One Hand Clapping*, includes Italian phrases in his Slovenian, Tasmanian and American vocabulary. For example, Bojan speaks the Italian phrase "Madonna Santa" (389), incomplete drunkenness, which means good gods. Nevertheless, there is no effect of the accent of the Italian language on the other languages that he uses.

> "*... he was back in the FJ and the motor was misfiring and rattling as he was driving into the heart of the town., and he was just hoping to Christ that it got him there and praised it in Slovenian (Dobra staryr auto) for all its years of faithful service and beseeched it in Italian (Perfavore cara macchina) to last the few more miles that would see their journey finally ended and ordered it on Deutsch (Raus! Raus!) to continue going and cursed it in Australian (shitfuckingbucket) for spluttering worse than himself in the morning. (412)*"

This balanced mixture of the languages of various cultures shows the orthogonal, that is non-related, nature of belongingness to more than one culture. Bojan's adoption of languages, a part of various cultures, does not affect his association or identification with other cultures. Flanagan can be said to have represented all sects of society in his works through the variety of characters that are lively and relatable for the readers. He represents the different types of universal migrants, but he also beautifully portrays the psychological and social implications of two or more cultures interacting.

In his research paper entitled 'A critical examination of acculturation theories,' Hieu Van Ngo has discussed various theories on acculturation in three different phases. In the first phase, the theories were 'Unidirectional' in which all the theories were only about the absorption of the less dominant or the non-dominant groups into the dominant culture, basically talking about assimilation. The major theorists in this phase were Gordon, Gans, Portes, and Zhou. Gordon was the most prominent one who classified assimilation into seven types, out of which he considered 'structural assimilation' to be the most important one. According to him, structural assimilation is when there is a large-scale entrance into the institutions of the dominant culture. He opined that when structural assimilation takes place, the other six types of assimilation automatically follow. According to Ngo, the primary issue in this unidirectional school of thought was a monolithic view of culture. Only the immigrants have to change and leave their culture when the dominant culture comes into the picture. The second phase discussed by Ngo is Bidimensional Acculturation. Unidirectional acculturation had many loopholes, and its criticism led to the birth of theories that dealt with and discussed both the cultures involved. An essential theorist that has given the base to the theory of Acculturation is JW Berry. He gave a quadric-modal of acculturation, talking about all the possibilities of the interaction of two cultures. The four strategies that Berry gave were assimilation, separation, marginalization, and integration. Apart from Berry, other scholars and theorists also gave their perception of acculturation from the perspective of both cultures, like J. Phinney in 1990 and Y R. Bouris, LC. Moise, S. Perrault and S. Senecal in 1997.

The researcher in '*Acculturation: A review of the literature* has focused on communication as an underlying factor and the outcome of the process of acculturation. He has reviewed the research that has been done in the field of acculturation, beginning with Redfield, Linton, and Herskovits 1936 definition of acculturation. He has stated that there has been much research done in this area since the 1930s, and there are many models given by various scholars. However, very few of them considered communication a vital part of this process where a stranger has to contact the host culture. He talked about Young Kim in detail as the latter has considered communication an essential part of the acculturation process and has done detailed and in-depth research. He has defined acculturation from the angle of communication, something that was not ever done before. Lakey also states that with JW Berry stepping into this area of research, it became more of a psychological stance. He concludes his essay by stating- "Much of the acculturation process is adapting to and adopting central rules and patterns of communication of the host culture. The immigrant's communication competence facilitates all other aspects of adjustment in the host environment." (16)

In '*Psychological aspects of cultural pluralism: unity and identity reconsidered*,' Berry talks about the plurality or diversity of cultures in every society or nation. This plurality is sometimes accepted and sometimes is a problem when the government tries to implement a policy on the nation without paying heed to the needs and the aims of a variety of cultures surviving together. Considering the Canadian government to be the best in accepting this plurality in the nation, he wants Africa and the rest of the third world nations to adopt the same schemes as the Canadian government. Berry talks about the issue of unity and identity concerning the nation-state. He answers three crucial questions that are likely to arise in this whole acculturation process with eight patterns of answers. The three questions taken up by him are-

1. Whether the immigrant maintains his own culture or not?
2. Whether he maintains a good relationship with the host society or not?
3. Whether it is his choice to choose the answer for the first two questions or not?

He concludes his paper by saying that every nation must have unity but not at the cost of reducing identity or freedom of choice as that cost would look easier to pay now but will be too great in the long run. In the following table, he has given names to all the possibilities that can arise after these three questions are answered-

QUESTION 1	QUESTION 2	QUESTION 3	PATTERN	
Retention of Identity?	Positive Relations?	Choice by Ethnic Group?	Number	Name
"YES"	"YES"	"YES"	1	Integration (Democratic Pluralism)
		"NO"	2	Paternal Integration (Inclusive segregation)
	"NO"	"YES"	3	Rejection (Self-segregation)
		"NO"	4	Exclusive Segregation
"NO"	"YES"	"YES"	5	Assimilation 1 (Melting pot)
		"NO"	6	Assimilation 2 (Pressure cooker)
	"NO"	"YES"	7	Marginality
		"NO"	8	Deculturation

Figure 2 : Berry J.W., "Psychological aspects of cultural pluralism: unity and identity reconsidered." Topics in culture learning 2 (1974): 17-22.

Bency and Baiju have examined the prevalent theories and models of acculturation, intending to investigate the patterns of acculturation followed by the immigrants that undergo this process. They focused mainly on how the immigrants engage themselves in the process of acculturation and the pattern of stress and challenges they face during the process. At the same time, they get placed in a new and strange culture unknown to them. The scholars have also given the gist of the four strategies given by Berry and Sam in their paper which was published in 1997. Joy and Gopal have observed that the strategies may differ from each other depending upon various factors like age, gender, familial and structural resources, the period of stay, the quality of the relationship established between the people who have migrated and hence now belong to the minority culture and the people of the majority of the dominant culture. (9)

In a chapter, ' acculturation and psychological adaptation: An overview' in the book titled 'Journeys into Cross-Cultural Psychology,' Berry states that acculturation and adaptation take place at two levels: individual level and group level. Acculturation on an individual level may have three folds-Adjustment, Reaction, and Withdrawal. Berry states that Psychological acculturation, as discussed by Graves in 1967, is an alternate word for acculturation where the former is for individual level and the latter for the group-level. Berry then talks about the four strategies that an individual or a group of immigrants might opt for while undergoing the process of acculturation. These are assimilation, segregation, integration, and marginalization. Later in the chapter, while talking about the behavioral shifts because of the contact with a new culture, Berry names the two phenomenons that could occur later in the process of acculturation. One is learning behaviors from the new cultures, and the other is shedding features of one's original cultures. Finally, he says that the process of acculturation gives birth to acculturative stress and after the combined review of the literature with Kim in 1988, concludes that problems arise during the process of acculturation, whether the problems will lead to the life of the immigrant or will end it, will depend on the relation between the acculturation and the stress of that individual or group. In a paper published in 2006, Berry has conducted a survey taking up the samples from 13 different countries that take up the most significant number of immigrants. The total number of participants was seven thousand nine hundred ninety-seven adolescents. There were five thousand three hundred and sixty-six immigrant youth and two thousand six hundred and thirty-one national youth. The main aim of conducting this survey was to answer three questions. First, how does the youth, that constitutes the majority part of a nation's population, deals with the process of acculturation? Second, how well do they accept and merge into this sort of circumstance? Third, is there any relationship between the first two questions?

Padilla, in his '*Acculturation, social identity, and social cognition: A new perspective*,' gives a new perspective or vision to the theories and models of acculturation that were already established. In order to achieve his goal, he starts his research paper by giving a summary of all the papers published till the date of writing of this paper about the option chosen by the immigrants to acculturate and its effects and causes. He begins with Robert Park, who initiated this study and, drawing on the ecological framework, gave a three-stage model considered the hallmark of the Chicago School of Sociology-contact, accommodation, and assimilation. Park was followed by Redfield et al., who brought the psychological aspect to the ecological framework of Park and gave a proper definition to the concept of acculturation. Finally, he describes Berry's four-fold model of acculturation, its limit, and all the models to date. According to Padilla, all the existent theories and models fail to address the individual differences that play a vital role in acculturation. The model of Padilla is based on four essential terms, which are interrelated and, according to Padilla, are the four pillars of his model. These are social cognition, cultural competence, social identity, and social stigma. Social cognition is the mental or intellectual capability of the immigrants to adapt to the various features of the host society. Cultural competence is the capability that enables the individual to get mixed up with the larger or majority culture. Social identity is what is visible about the individual as a member of the dominant group. Social stigma is showing or hiding the attributes every individual holds that could make the person stigmatized in the eyes of the dominant society. Showing or hiding these attributes is a matter of individual differences.

The Trauma of Immigration and the Ethics of Self-Positioning in Richard Flanagan's 'The Sound of One Hand Clapping' elaborates the traumatic experience of the people who were a part of postwar immigration to Australia to start a new life as shown by Flanagan in his novel 'The Sound of One Hand Clapping.' This novel revolves around Buloh family members and their experience of dealing with this trauma. Bojan Buloh, the protagonist's father, and Sonja, the protagonist, are the center of the discussion. The writer of 'To voice or not to Voice the Tasmanian Aborigines: Novels by

Matthew Kneale and Richard Flanagan' has compared the setting, approach, and narrative strategies of two prize-winning novels- Kneale's English Passengers and Richard Flanagan's Gould's Book of Fish. The people have been silenced over the time due to various known reasons. However, this paper observes that these two writers, as mentioned above, try to give voice to these silenced people, which has been done till now, neither by the contemporary writers nor by the non-contemporary writers. These writers did something unique by giving identity to these marginalized people while also following all the set stereotypes. In Colonial Desire and the Renaming of History in Richard Flanagan's *Wanting*, the writer examines the psychological impact and the physical violence that comes along with colonialism as represented in Flanagan's novel *Wanting*. The writer winds up his paper, with a statement, saying, Flanagan investigates the correlation between colonialism and post-colonialism, civilization and savagery, fiction and reality, and by doing so he reshapes history by revealing the deficient elements in colonial conversation.

In 'Representation of War in Richard Flanagan's *The Narrow Road to the Deep North*,' the writer analyzed the representation of war in Flanagan's novel The Narrow Road to the Deep North. It critically analyses the psychological aspect or the effects of the incidents with Dorrigo Evans, the lead character, a survivor of the less known Burma Death Railway. The writer in 'Submerging the imperial eye: Affective narration as an environmentalist intervention in Richard Flanagan's *Death of a River Guide*,' pronounces that Flanagan has his narrator to critique the imperial eye and the rationalist construction of the human that it exhibits, divulging their involvement in strengthening a hallucination of human separation from non-human nature that has disastrous environmental repeat percussions. The writer of this article concludes that through the character of Gould, Flanagan ironically suggests the basic human tendency that a human being behaves most truthfully when he realizes and accepts the lies that he lives with and that too with complete honesty. The novel reveals the way that history has been manipulated by the hands of those who were powerful and those who wrote history. The novelist very cleverly depicts that those who try to point a figure towards the creation process of history meet a fatal end, which is valid in all the time zones of past and present.

The writer of this article winds up by saying that Sir John and Dickens give in to their immoral lust for girls, which resultantly marks them as anthropophagus savages in the novel. Through this, Flanagan questions the masculinized colonial project, primarily as the characters represent Britain and the Empire. It is generally observed that many people fantasize the epic battles. However, this article aims to blemish the mass opinion about the fantasies of epic battles and restructure them by bringing out the reality of the POW's camp and how they are presented. The writer of this paper analyses the two crime fiction novels and concludes that, like the conventional convict novel, their aim to redraft the settler narrative has been weakened by longing for the past that that story presents. Inventing the Past: Regional Myth in Michael Crummey's Galore and Richard Flanagan's Gould's Book of Fish investigated how these authors have used myth and history to investigate the effects of these forged narratives about the past on identity formation in the present. Living Conditions in Van Diemen's Land in Clarke's For the Term of His Natural Life and Flanagan's Gould's Book of Fish compared the narrative strategies and the portrayal of the main characters by Clarke and Flanagan in their books 'For the Term of His Natural Life' and The Gould's Book of Fish' and how they depict the convict life.

The Perils of Translation: The demonstration of Australian Cultural Identity in the French Translations of Crime Fiction Novels of Richard Flanagan and Philip McLaren made a comparative textual study of four crime fiction novels by two widely known Australian authors, Richard Flanagan and Philip McLaren, in which the two authors have intentionally aimed at creating a unique sense of Australian cultural identity. It also presents the vulnerability of the techniques used by the people in the field of translation. Littoral Fictions: Writing Tasmania and Newfoundland analyzed contemporary literary fiction that takes either the Canadian island of Newfoundland or the Australian island of Tasmania as its ingenious ground or setting. It reported that Newfoundland and Tasmania play vital roles within the storyline depending upon the alternate geographical routes it spots. The objectives of the research are:

- To understand acculturation and its processes

- To study cultural identity and identification

- To explore intricacies of acculturation in the fiction of Richard Flanagan

- To trace the orthogonal cultural identification in the works of Richard Flanagan
- To apply the theory of acculturation and orthogonal cultural identification.

The study will explore the fiction of Richard Flanagan concerning acculturation and orthogonal cultural identification theories. The study will seek to bring out the aspects of the culture and the identity of the characters being influenced by two or more cultures coming together, as depicted by Richard Flanagan in his novels. The texts will be critically analyzed using qualitative research to foreground the effects of two cultures coming in contact. It will be a thematic study of the selected works concerning the emerging trends of acculturation and orthogonal cultural identification. The study will also explore the intricacies of the social and psychological implications of the acculturation and orthogonal cultural identification processes by analyzing the characters' lives that represent the sections or the types of the people who migrate to a society where two or more than two cultures co-exist.

CHAPTER TWO

Assimilation and Integration

Assimilation is a process in which two individuals, groups, cultures, parties, or objects come in contact and the one with a weak back or base merges in the strong one losing its own identity. Assimilation is sub-divided into six categories- Color assimilation, Cultural assimilation, Religious assimilation, Linguistic assimilation, Psychological assimilation, and Statistical assimilation. J. W. Berry, in 1994, stated that the effects of interaction between two cultures could be seen at two levels- Individual and Group. Talking about the individual level, he suggested that an immigrant adopts any of the three strategies when s/he comes in contact with native culture- *adjustment, reaction,* and *withdrawal.* If he chooses to adjust, s/he fits into the native culture without affecting the latter. In the reaction strategy, the immigrant takes the help of the campaigns to make specific changes in the native culture that makes her/his survival in a new culture easier. In the option of withdrawal, the immigrant fails to survive in the new culture and return to the culture of origin.

Cultural assimilation is when an individual or a group interacting with another individual or group resembles a powerful individual or group. In this process, the person from a minority culture or the minority group loses the culture of origin and adopts the native culture. In his paper published in 1998, Berry suggested that it is one of the aspects of the acculturation process, and it has now become one of the phases of acculturation. The term assimilation is usually confused with acculturation. However, the difference is apparent: acculturation is an umbrella term whereas assimilation is a part or a phase of acculturation that an immigrant undergoes. At the same time, s/he comes in contact with a new and dominant culture. There are various definitions of assimilation-

According to Robert E. Park and Ernest W. Burgess, social behavior has four categories out of which assimilation is one and the three others being conflict, accommodation, and competition. It is "a process of interpenetration and fusion in which person and groups acquire the memories, sentiments, and attitudes of other person or groups and share their experience and history are incorporated into everyday cultural life." (735) E.C Parsons differentiated between acculturation and assimilation stating that the former is a unidirectional process while the latter is a two-way process (213). Carrying it further, Hirsch, in 1942 argued that assimilation should not be mistaken as a concept that can be further bifurcated. However, it is a dynamic process that has various degrees to it.

J. W. Berry suggested that if an individual or a group of individuals come in contact with a foreign person or group where the culture of the latter is accepted in the majority, then the former person or group will have four ways to react to the new culture. He termed them as strategies- Assimilation, Integration, Separation, and Marginalization. Mentioning assimilation, he stated that it is a process in which the immigrant has very little interest in maintaining his own culture and believes in accepting the majority's culture. In 1992, J. W. Berry gave two types of assimilation based on answers to three questions- Does the immigrant retains her/his identity? Does s/he look forward to maintaining positive relations with the native culture? Does the ethnic group make a choice? He termed assimilation1 as melting pot and assimilation2 as pressure cooker. Giving the example of Irish immigrants migrating to the United States, Berry says that there are still many cases where the immigrants voluntarily choose to adopt the native culture, which is melting pot's case. Answering the three questions, Berry defines the melting pot as the process in which the immigrant group chooses to maintain positive relations with the native culture and not to retain their own culture. Talking about melting pot, he says that it is a voluntary action on the part of the immigrants where "...whenever an immigrant group accepts the goals of the new society and is willing to adopt the patterns of the new society to attain the goals" (19).

The second type of assimilation is pressure cooker, in which the decision to leave one's own culture and adopt the native culture is forced instead of it being voluntary. According to Berry, in 1974, this type of assimilation is still prevalent in relations between the whites and the aborigines in Australia. Pressure cooker can also be called 'forced assimilation'. In an educational video on YouTube titled '*Lecture 11- Acculturation, Assimilation and Integration*', the speaker suggested that assimilation is the process in which two cultures come together, borrow and mix up with the native culture so much so that they lose their identity and come up with a new identity altogether. She gives an example of the Indians shifting to America, where the Indians first adopt consumption and dressing patterns. Slowly, with time, they lose their Indian identity and take up a new identity (00:07:45 - 00:08:31).

Out of the four strategies of acculturation, integration is the second one. Unlike assimilation, integration is positive. In the former process, the immigrants leave their origin and adopt the native culture either voluntarily or by force, whereas, in the latter process, the immigrants carry both cultures. This process is the most common strategy found globally as the immigrants can enjoy values, customs, and traditions of both the cultures. In the educational video on YouTube titled 'Lecture 11- Acculturation, Assimilation and Integration', the speaker suggests that integration happens when the two different entities come in contact with each other, and society tends to force them to work together the society needs to grow. According to her, the society grows from homogeneous to heterogeneous (00:13:45 - 00:14:15). Talking about the factors that influence the process of integration, she considers the size of the group to be the most important factor because if the size of the group is small, the integration would be faster compared to a large group in which it is sometimes impossible to integrate. The second factor that she mentions is that for successful integration, face-to-face interaction is significant (00:19:57 - 00:20:48).

John W. Berry has given a four-fold model of acculturation, stated that the Canadian Government promotes integration. According to him, there are two types of integration- democratic pluralism and paternal integration. According to him, the Canadian Government promotes the first one that is democratic pluralism. Based on the answers to the three questions mentioned earlier, he states that in democratic pluralism, it is the choice of the ethnic group to maintain positive relations with the native culture and retain their own culture of origin. They are free to choose the option of integration without any external or internal force or pressure on them. According to him, Switzerland is a perfect example of democratic pluralism. Elaborating on the second type of integration, Berry, in 1974, stated that it is not the choice of the ethnic group to carry both cultures together in this type. Hence, he gave another term to this type that is inclusive segregation. The dominant culture decides that positive relations with the dominant culture and the original ethnicity are to be maintained as it is the need of the dominant society and not the choice of the immigrants. In his words-

"This pattern usually requires an efficient set of social- control agents (e.g., police or passes) for its enforcement." (19)

Integration is possible in a pluralistic society and both groups are equally positive in successful interaction. However, even if the dominant culture is ready to integrate, the immigrants hesitate to come forward and show a positive reaction. There can be many reasons out of which the physical features according to Berry et al. in 1989 have played a significant role. Various studies have been conducted in this area. Many studies have shown that integration is preferred over other three strategies given by Berry. However, there are a few exceptions also. For example, Turks in Germany (Piontkowski, Florack, Hoelker, & Obdrzalek 20) and lower socioeconomic status Turks in Canada (Berry, Kwak & Ataca 76) choose to separate themselves rather than integration.

J.W. Berry also studied larger societies and changed the names of the strategies concerning the size of the society.

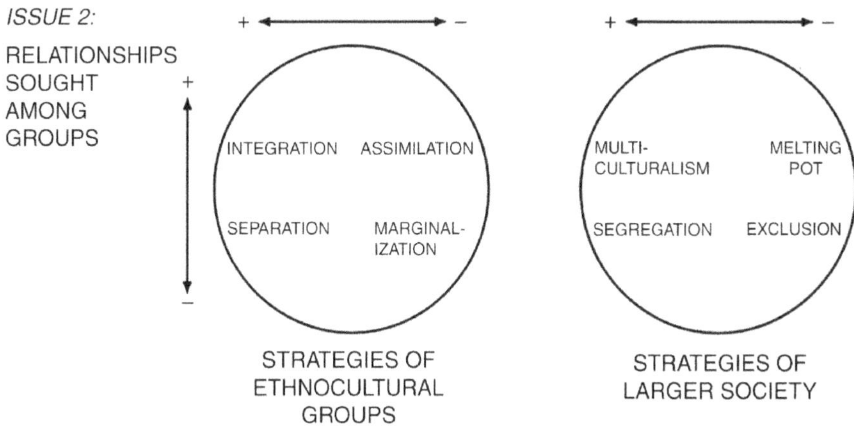

Figure 3 : Berry J.W., "A psychology of immigration." *Journal of social issues* **57.3 (2001): 615-631.**

Multiculturalism is the strategy of cooperation and accommodation. The dominant culture is liberal enough to accept the existence of norms, values, traditions, etc., of various other cultures with its own. Thus, the dominant society plays a vital role in maintaining cultural diversity in a multicultural society. Even the cultures of the minority have a positive outlook and a liberal attitude towards a culturally diverse society. Berry's views suggest that multiculturalism corresponds to integration as shown in the picture above. However, it comes closer to the term *separation* and not to *integration* because it has 'us-them feeling in the communities and hence can trigger the differences rather than integrating. (Kagitcibasi 44). However, in the latest studies of plural societies, it is believed that it is now like a balance. According to Watts and Smolicz, it is a very flexible framework for all the cultures that make up one country. In 1997, Berry stated that integration and assimilation had been used interchangeably for more than two decades. However, these two are different and hence proposes two further divisions of each. Richard Flanagan's fiction will hence be analyzed based on Berry's division of these two pillars of acculturation.

Richard Flanagan has portrayed both types of assimilation very well. In *First Person*, the narrator Kif is born in Tasmania, but he knows nothing much about its history, values, and traditions. He shifts to Melbourne to write the biography of a criminal, Ziggy Heidl and assimilates into the culture of that city with his own will (16). This was precisely the idea of Berry behind the theory of *Melting Pot*. Ziggy Heidl was born in South Australia but moves to Germany when he turns 26. He adopts the German accent forgetting the accent of his mother tongue that he used for the first 26 years (5). He is the perfect example of melting pot, in which the immigrant or the person from the minority culture melts down entirely in the native culture or the culture of the majority with his own will without experiencing any sort of internal or external force or pressure. There can be various reasons that can result in assimilation, like the birth of hatred in the hearts of the immigrants for their culture of origin and the fascination or attraction of immigrants towards the native culture. The blacks or the aborigines of Australia are fascinated by the color of the skin of whites that they even start touching their skin and admire almost everything the white people do (56). Ray, the narrator's friend, also moves out for work and becomes one of the others and as a result, starts hating the culture of origin and the people related to that culture. He abuses Tasmanians, calling them ''shit-eaters'' and ''two-headed'' (213), which shows that he has no interest in maintaining the culture of origin. Ray considered himself to belong to an inferior culture and hence said, "...we are nothing. What did Nietzsche or Tebbe or, for that matter, the world of publishing, know about shit eating?"

The Sound of One Hand Clapping is also a text that is full of instances of assimilation. This text has a non-linear structure as the chapters of this novel move between different years. It begins in 1954 when Sonja, the protagonist, was three years old, and in 1989, she turns thirty-nine. In between, the story also revolves around Sonja when she celebrates her sixteenth birthday in 1967. It is said that the parents play a vital role in deciding the offspring's decisions. In the novel, Maria Buloh, mother of the three-year-old protagonist Sonja, tells her the importance of adopting the native culture while talking to her daughter. Sonja asks Maria why they have tea. Replying to her daughter's question, Maria says they are in Tasmania and not in Slovenia, and their world is upside down (31). She further says- "... to have a future, you must forget the past, my little knedel." (31)

Bojan Bulah, the protagonist's father, chooses to speak in English and not his mother tongue. Although his English was broken, he still prefers English over Slovenian. However, with time and her parents' efforts, Sonja becomes fluent in spoken English. Once, he says, "Yeh, we Aussies are never late." (32) Even when he is alone, he tries to introspect in broken English and not his mother tongue (110). This is an indicator of the fact that he wants to assimilate, and there is no internal or external pressure on him. In 1954, when Sonja is three years old, Bojan talks in "rolling Slovenian" (213), but now he speaks in English, although it does not sound smooth (213). He feels proud to speak English and associate him with Australia as if it had always been his dream to become an Australian. He owns a car that he names as 'FJ' in Australia and once says to his daughter, "... it was a proof to both those in Slovenia and Australia that he had become what he had set out to be: Australian." (85)

It has been a story of almost every immigrant who migrated to a foreign land, utterly unknown to them, to get a better future. Bojan Buloh and Maria Buloh also migrate from Slovenia to Australia to improve the chances of a better future for them and their daughter Sonja. They plan to "forget the past" (31), including the country and culture of origin and the language of origin. In an attempt to fulfill their dream, Bojan brings 'Encyclopedia-bloody-Britannica" (215) so that their daughter becomes fluent in the native language that is English. Giving the book to Sonja, Bojan says, "Now you learn the English good." He feels proud of the fact that his daughter will now be fluent in English (215). Bojan is so attracted to the native language and is so willing to be one of the natives that even when his daughter Sonja says, in Slovenian, "Adio, Artie", meaning goodbye, Bojan replies in

English (319). Sonja, with time, learns the language and culture of Australia. She makes Australian food and feels proud to have done that- "...standing in an apron serving the Australian meal, which she was so proud to have prepared." (200)

A few characters in *The Narrow Road to the Deep North* adopt the native language and culture without pressure. The novel deals with the breathtaking and pathetic condition of the prisoners of war from various countries. These prisoners have been kept in Japanese POW Camps and are assigned to build Railway tracks for the Japanese. They struggle from starvation, death, diseases, and beatings from the Japanese officers. Colonel Rexroth, an Australian, who becomes one of the POWs, chooses to speak in English. He strives to be mistaken as English. He believes that he is English and proudly calls himself a British. Talking to the protagonist Dorrigo, he once says, "... he believed that all their British national strengths would be enough, that their British esprit de corps would hold, and their British spirit would not break, and their British blood would bring them through it together." (43) He considers himself British to the extent that he ascends the stage and starts giving a motivational speech to other POWs. "... And for that reason, as members of the British Empire, as Englishmen, we must observe order and discipline that is the very lifeblood of the empire. We will suffer as Englishmen, we will triumph as Englishmen. Thank you." (46) Choi Sang-min adopts the way the Japanese behave with the prisoners and behaves in the same way. He somehow gets some authority over the prisoners even when he is Korean and not Japanese. He beats the already suffering prisoners just because it is the Japanese way of treating them. He willingly adopts the Japanese ways as they are in the majority (323).

There are elements of assimilation by own will or *Melting Pot* in all the fictional works by Richard Flanagan. *The Unknown Terrorist* also has a few instances. The Doll is the protagonist of the novel. She works as a prostitute. She is an Australian and also a black, but she never lets her complexion affect her lifestyle. She is a blind follower of brands and thus improves her living standard; she pretends to be of an elite white class. Everything she owns is a brand, and she earns money to buy a branded bag that she always wanted to buy. She visits her mother occasionally, who is always less interested in the Doll but is influenced by her sons, who are influenced by the American style of speaking and dressing. "... mother talked only of her two sons, two fat boys who dressed like two fat rappers, said *Yo* a lot and greeted each other American style, rubbing fist knuckles... (8) She adopts white Australian's lifestyle, so much so that she starts hating the black woman and ''her blackness'', whom she meets in the park." (224)

Richard Flanagan's subsequent work of fiction *Wanting* revolves around a black aborigine girl and her struggles as she moves to the majority's culture and back to her own culture. She is fascinated by the native culture so much that she starts putting effort into learning English. As she moves out of her culture of origin with Mr. John and Lady Jane, she is trained to live as white people lived. After a few days of hard training, Mathinna feels comfortable in the new environment. The servant finds "... the black girl and the white possum, both asleep." (224) At this turn of the plot, the togetherness of black and white is a metaphor of assimilation, meaning that the black is comfortable with the white and is in complete harmony. Before Mathinna is taken to the white society, she seems to be fond of red so much that she wants everything belonging to her to be red. However, then she is taken away from her culture of origin and is trained for better behavior. The moment she starts feeling comfortable, her choices begin to change, and as a result, she starts dressing up like French aristocrats, as is wanted by the majority's culture (130). Mathinna even starts criticizing the servants with whom she has always been shy even to talk, adopting the way to behave with them from the whites (133).

In an aristocratic party, Mathinna does not behave the way she was expected to behave. She is appropriately dressed and also talks the way she should, according to the whites. However, when dancing on stage, she starts English but flows to her origin with the flow. After this incident, Lady Jane decides to send her to an orphanage as the former thinks she cannot assimilate to their culture and never learn what they are trying to teach her. Nevertheless, Mathinna's desire to be one of the whites is never suppressed, even after being sent to the orphanage and all the bad behavior. She returns to her native place, but she faces many issues adjusting with them as she grows habitual to the white way of life, and now she wants to go back to that society all the way more.

Mathinna starts writing a diary because she has always seen Lady Jane regularly write to impress McMohan (215). She desires to be seen as one of the whites when she uses English to write the diary over her mother tongue. McMahan reads her diary in which he finds is full of errors and broken English-

"They should not throw about the soap they have too much the soap is fine thing to wash yourselves with and yet they don't care for it, no they would sooner put on that there red clayey stuff what they have being always used and they like it better than soap to their faces. (216)"

When the black women gather and do the devil dance, which is local to their culture of origin, Mathinna wants to tell the women that they are "uncivilized and uncouth" and she behaves with them as the whites behaved. This behavior or thought process is just a glimpse of her inner desire to be seen as one of the whites and an aristocrat (217). Mathinna, then unable to cope with the stress, turns to prostitution to earn a good amount of money, but then also she criticizes the blacks and talks like Lady Jane used to talk. She calls people of her tribe as "stinking no-good stupid blackfellas," and on realizing that she is not with Lady Jane and is not standing in the Government House, she adds "... these no-good, good for nothing savages who knew nowt." (244) Mathinna tells Walter Talba Bruney, a black companion, that she does not belong to these black people but is white and her life will be great, just like white people in the future. She says "... I no savage or slave. Them no-good lazy blackfellas, they disgust me. I marry a whitefella, you watch, you see, I be big lady. (246) She uses English with Walter Talba Bruney, with whom she could have used her native language. Moreover, she does not seem to be affected if her English is broken.

Death of a River Guide revolves around the protagonist Aljaz, who works as a river guide and is drowning at the beginning of the novel and is granted visions. As he lies drowning, he sees the history of three generations- Ned Quade (his grandfather), Harry (his father), and his own life running as a picture in front of his eyes. As the novel begins, Aljaz tells the story of his birth at the hands of an Italian lady Maria Magdalena Svevo. Maria migrates to Australia in search of work. There she helps Sonja in giving birth to Aljaz. Aljaz feels proud of not knowing anything about his own culture and his own country. (96) Harry, the protagonist's father and an Australian, meets Auntie Ellie, who is an aborigine. Auntie Ellie does not consider herself a black aborigine, but she believes herself to be decent white catholic folk. When Harry asks her whether she is an aborigine or not, she scolds him and says, "Don't you go talking about decent people in that sort of way? It does no good, you hear? We are good decent Catholic folk, good decent white Catholic folk, you understand?" (201) However, Harry, not agreeing with her, further discusses the same topic, she starts slapping him, and with every slap, she stresses that they are not "Abos" and belong to the decent white Catholic folk. She hates the culture of her origin and wants to be recognized as the colonizers who are large in number and want every aborigine to adopt their way of life to be more in number (202).

By birth, Sonja, Aljaz's mother, is from Yugoslavia but marries Harry, an Australian. She gets assimilated by her own will. She starts liking 'Nescaf'e,' which is liked by Australians (247). Apart from the central characters, other ordinary people of Tasmania are also attracted by the British culture and the possibilities of a better future if they leave their culture of origin and migrate to a foreign land. In a song sung by the aborigine rock band, we come to know that there is a minor character Shag, whose sister calls Tasmania as hell and leaves the country (259). Psychology of Shag's sister is similar to all those who come in contact with the majority's culture. People of minority cultures adopt the values and lifestyle of the majority's culture by their own will.

In *Gould's Book of fish*, the second narrator and the character in the title William Buelow Gould is a convict of British colonizers and is kept in Van Dieman's Land, now known as Tasmania. He is assigned a task to use his painting skills and paint a book of fish. Many minor characters around him decide with their own will to leave their culture of origin and adopt the British culture of whites or the majority's culture. Although William Buelow Gould is a white man, he is a captive or a prisoner. The black aborigines leave their culture and country for exile and leave themselves at the will of the whites. Their submission to the whites gives them superiority over the whites who are prisoners. The convicts feel the superiority expressed by the savages, and the formers believe, "... some convicts in the Penitentiary pissed through the boards on the savages housed on the floor below us to prove the superiority of an imprisoned white man over an exiled black man." (216)

Guster Robinson is a white conciliator who considers the blacks as his associates. Nevertheless, the savages, who have left their fates on the will of the whites, consider Robinson as "one of the many stray dogs they picked up on the travels." (217) The savages do so because the whites do not have a good image of Robinson amongst them as the latter has always been a supporter of the blacks. The savages, as they work according to the whites, choose to act like whites of their own will. These savages melt in the new culture without any internal or external pressure.

In 1974, Berry gave another type of assimilation: *Pressure Cooker*, in which the culture of the minority is forced by external or internal pressure to assimilate in the culture of the majority. Some characters in the fiction of Richard Flanagan are forced to forget their culture of origin and adopt the native culture. In *Gould's Book of Fish,* Brady forces and turns the savages and the convicts upside-down to change Van Dieman's Land into a new world in an imitation of England (197). Twopenny Sal is pressured by the white people who land in Australia, searching for servants. They kidnap Twopenny Sal's son and promise to give her son back only if she agrees to come to the land of Whites and be a part of their culture by being their maidservant. Due to the lack of options, she leaves her land and culture behind. Moreover, as a result, slowly, with time, she assimilates into the new culture, giving birth to the children of her owners. This painful life experience of Twopenny Sal is worth noticing as to how the dominant culture, with money and power, forced the weak people from a minority culture.

Kif in *First Person* is the narrator and the protagonist who is assigned a task to write the biography of a criminal, Heidl. Ray, Kif's friend, is somehow forced to work with the criminal. Ray wants to be free as a bird. He behaves as if he is a French aristocrat. He fights and struggles inside him. Kif says, "... I could see he was engaged in a mysterious battle between his desire to be free and where that desire had now led him- servitude to a monster." (155) This extract shows that Ray is under some pressure, due to undefined circumstances, to work with the criminal Heidl. Similarly, in *The Sound of One Hand Clapping*, the politician pressures immigrants to assimilate into the Australian culture. He gives false hopes to the immigrants about their future. Immigrants are sad to leave the culture of origin, but they are pressured and call it necessary. By promising a better tomorrow than their lives in the past, the immigrants are psychologically pressurized by the politician of Australia who wants them to forget their past to enter in a new and a better version of their poor lives.

For the Australian officials the naturalization ceremony was a joyous, celebratory moment when the new Australians renounced their previous citizenship- their country, their past- to become Australians. For those being naturalized it was a sad but necessary step to take. (42) Bojan, the protagonist Sonja's father, listens to the promises made by the politician when suddenly he realizes that the three-year-old Sonja grasps his finger.

When he thinks about Sonja and her future, he is bound to take this decision to assimilate and behave as the Australians do for the betterment of his little daughter. Having these thoughts in mind, Bojan feels sad about his country, culture and heavy- heartedly take this tough decision. "...it seemed as if his arm were in another country that he was leaving forever and to which he might never be allowed to return." (43)

Further, in order to influence and psychologically pressurize the immigrants, the politician tells the immigrants that they need to bring the determination to be like the Australians. They will get the most expensive gift of being a part of English culture and learning English (44). By telling the superiority of the English language and English culture, the politician makes the immigrants feel wrong about their culture of origin and proud of the culture they will assimilate. There are other pressures also apart from psychological pressure. Social pressure is one of them. Under the social pressure, there is a fear of self-image in the society where all the neighbors of the Bojan family are Australian. Heaney's family is also one of the Australian families who live near Sonja's house. The former family is very influential and this creates social pressure on Bojan. When Sonja serves the food that Heaneys eat, Bojan does not like it, but he asks Sonja whether she is sure about the food habits of Heaneys. When Sonja confirms it, Bojan starts eating the food and pretends to like it, but he curses the Australians' eating styles and eating habits (201). Under the same social pressure, Bojan indirectly pressurizes Sonja to learn the English language so that she does not end up like her father, saying that although English is "no good for jokes," it is "good for money." (214)

The Narrow Road to the Deep North is a novel full of violence by the Japanese authority on the POWs (Prisoners of war) from different countries. A Japanese officer climbs up the tree stump and starts addressing the prisoners. In order to indirectly influence the prisoners, he expresses the superiority of Japan and asks the prisoners to feel proud as they are serving the Japanese (41). Nakamura, one of the Japanese characters in the novel, also pressurizes the prisoners indirectly by boasting about the plans of Japan behind the wars- "the whole world under one roof, (115) indirectly telling them that the whole world will one day be like Japan and forget its existence. This phrase has been the strategy of every culture in the majority to directly or indirectly create pressure on the immigrants or the people of minority culture to make them assimilate in the majority culture and leave their culture and country somewhere behind. There is no role of the immigrant's will in deciding this type of assimilation.

Auntie Ellie in *Death of a River Guide* slaps Harry repeatedly to make him agree on a statement that is not true. They are Aborigines, but she forces him to repeat that they are not abs but belong to decent white catholic folk. She is under immense pressure, which she shows by saying- "We ain't no Abos, we ain't no boongs, ya hear? Ya talk like that they'll take ya away, ya understand? They'll take ya back to the islands. I already told you what we are- decent white Catholic folk." (202) She fears that if the whites know that they are aborigines, the formers will take them away from their land. Under this pressure, she pressurizes Harry to say that they are decent white Catholic folk. Moreover, her language is also worth noticing. Using her mother tongue, she uses English calling Aborigines 'boongs' a derogatory term used by the whites.

Wanting is full of such instances that show that the people who belong to the minority culture in Australia are forced to forget their own culture and be like the people of the majority culture. However, the problem with this is that even if the people of minority culture adopt the majority culture and its lifestyle, they are not fully adopted by the majority culture and hence are left somewhere lurking in- between. Mathinna is the actual name of the little protagonist of the novel. The Protector, a white, is there to help the whites civilize the blacks in their mission to make every black like them and also helping the blacks to get a better lifestyle like the whites. He has changed the name of Mathinna to Leda as he christened her. The choice of the name Leda is related to ancient Greek mythology, in which Leda was raped by God Zeus in the form of a swan. It somehow shows the whites' mentality or psyche for the blacks relating them with something exotic and tempting. When Lady Jane mentions this mythology of Leda and the swan, the Protector says that they prefer to call her Mathinna (52).

The Protector is "weaning them off their native diet of berries and plants and shellfish and game" in the name of helping the Aborigines (2). He was playing with the psychology of the poor Aborigines. The latter are shifted to the terraces built by the Protector to "accustom them to English domesticity and to break them away from their rude windbreaks." (10) The wishes of the aborigines do not matter in any sense as their minds are being played with and they are made to believe that whatever the Protector id doing for them, it is for their good and the better future. The Protector influences the poor black natives and tries to convince the chief of the black aborigines, Towterer, father of Mathinna. The former creates mental pressure on Towterer, saying that they are to move to the island made by the whites for them. In exchange, "... they would be kept in food and provided with all the good things of the whites' world: clothing, shelter, tea, floor, God." (62) The white authorities believe that the 'few natives of the remotest wilds' (63) will be shifted to the island. For that matter, they are allowed to use any method for forcing the remaining natives to assimilate so that they do not have to fear the 'threat of the resurgent black natives.' (63)

Apart from other types of blackmail, emotional blackmail is also one of the weapons used in the novel by the whites to make the blacks agree with what they say. Robinson or the Protector adopts a similar technique to convince the chief of the black natives of Australia. Robinson has Towterer's daughter Mathinna who is already being trained by the whites, to be one of them. In her name, Robinson creates an emotional pressure on the chief to join her daughter in the English society if he wants his daughter back. This scene creates an external pressure on Towterer, but he knows that it is nothing more than a trick of Robinson and hence does not fall prey to him. Lady Jane orders her maid Widow Munro to nail close all the shutters of western windows to prevent the sight of woods from Mathinna's room. She does this to prevent any kind of painful nostalgia that Mathinna could otherwise experience seeing the woods as the latter might remember her home in the woods (115).

Mathinna wants to learn writing as she considers it some kind of magic that only whites know. Blackmailing her in the name of her dream to learn writing, Lady Jane forces Mathinna to wear shoes as Mathinna is not habitual. However, the society in which she is now shifted requires her to behave and dress in a particular manner. Lady Jane keeps a condition to give Mathinna pen and paper that the latter can have them only if she keeps on wearing shoes. Lady Jane wants to civilize Mathinna at any cost, and hence giving instructions to Widow Munro and forcing a smile on her face, Lady Jane says, "She will be shod and she will be civilized. And I trust you to ensure that both things happen." (117)

When Lady Jane realizes that she cannot train Mathinna, she sends her to an orphanage hostel that teaches and practices everything English society wanted- their lifestyle and religion. It is compulsory for everyone in the hostel to obey the rules and learn what is being taught. The routine life of the hostlers begins with the church and the church prayers, and they teach the orphans all about the lifestyle of the English. Moreover, those who do not follow the rules or fail to behave in the set format are punished with severe beatings repeatedly (119). Mathinna and Walter Talba Bruney are discovered sitting on the beech by McMohan. When McMohan arrives there, he finds Mathinna giving something to Walter Talba taken from her by another. The latter two decide that they do not want English people to rule over them. They would "live on their own wheat and potatoes their own muttonbirds and eggs and sheep." (185) On listening to them and on the sight he witnessed with his own eyes, McMohan trashes them and reminds them of the English religious teachings and asks them to fear the punishment of hell and fear from God. In order to save the damned soul of Mathinna, McMohan makes her his maid and sends Walter Talba Bruney to imprisonment for seven days (185).

All seven novels had the elements of assimilation. In some novels, the blacks assimilated to the culture of whites and, in some, the prisoners to the rulers. The assimilation can be seen of both types as is given by J.W. Berry in his work of 1974. In one type of assimilation, characters like Kif, Sonja, Colonel Rexroth, Choi Sang- min, the Doll, Mathinna, Maria, Auntie Ellie, etc. assimilate with the majority culture without their own will and no external or internal pressure. However, there are other characters like Harry, Ray, Walter Talba Bruney, Towterer, the minor PWs, Bojan, and the immigrants of Australia who are forced by the characters like Nakamura, the politician, the Japanese authorities, Lady Jane and the Protector or Robinson who create emotional, social or psychological pressure in order to make the people of minority culture assimilate with the people of the culture of the majority.

Integration can also be seen among the lives of various characters in the fiction of Richard Flanagan. J.W. Berry subdivided the strategy of integration into two types- Democratic pluralism and Parental integration. The difference is that the immigrants integrate both cultures in the former, and there is no pressure on them. However, in the latter, it is the wish of the majority culture that the immigrants or the people of minority culture maintain both the cultures well. The people of the majority culture usually use an agency to make sure that the rules of integration made in the dominant society are correctly followed. In all the seven novels of Richard Flanagan, various instances of Democratic pluralism can be seen easily.

It is usually said that children, compared to adults, can easily mix up well in a foreign culture, maintaining the culture of origin. Whereas, the adults of a minority culture face difficulty in adopting the traits of the majority culture as they have always been practicing one culture and that is the culture of origin throughout their lives. In *Death of a River Guide*, young Aljaz attempts to make other schoolboys accept him the way he is as he wants to carry both cultures together, leaving neither (90). As Aljaz grows up, he learns Italian phrases from Maria Magdalena, his midwife, who is Italian. Aljaz repeats "Madonna Santa!" (226), an Italian proverb that means 'Good Heavens.' However, Aljaz is an Australian and uses both Australian and Italian phrases. This integration of languages of two nations is on Aljaz's own will that is without any pressure. Apart from Aljaz, Maria Magdalena, Italian by birth, buys Australian cigars that she loves a lot. This mixing of two different cultures is also without any internal or external pressure. Reg, Auntie Ellie's husband, is an Australian aborigine who desires to complete his house with the popular construction material in America (193). The psyche of Reg shows that he is open- minded enough to carry two cultures without losing any one of them, and that too with his interests. These are the instances from *Death of a River Guide* that show the presence of Democratic pluralism in the minority culture.

In the novel *First Person*, there is a "Chimbu Lodge Disco," which is very traditional, but it is all western. Michel, Ray, and Kif reach the disco and see that the DJ is playing the Western songs that are Austrian and American and the bagpipes. The common thing that these three men find in the music is that all of it is western. The Chimbu men and women enjoy American songs. (56) There are many situations where Kif, the narrator and the protagonist of the novel, uses American proverbs even though he is an Australian and hence has the Australian accent to the English. The Australian people who enjoy the Western music sitting in the traditional Australian disco and Kif choose to integrate one or the other elements of another culture in the culture of origin. Similarly, the Doll, the protagonist of the novel *The Unknown Terrorist*, also chooses to be a combination of two different cultures on her own. She is an Australian and hence speaks English with an Australian touch to it. However, she runs after brands all the time. She works as a prostitute, but she saves her money from the beginning of the novel to buy a branded bag that she has had an eye on for a very long time. She has a black complexion, and with that, she desires to be seen as a rich westerner using all those brands in whatever she uses. Language is an essential aspect of a culture that an immigrant who desires to assimilate or integrate learns first. In the novel *The Narrow Road to the Deep North*, Fukuhara is a translator who works with Nakamura. Nakamura is Japanese, and Fukuhara, being Japanese, translates Nakamura's speech to English for the prisoners from various countries (216). The prisoners also integrate a common language apart from their mother tongue as the land. Apart from language, lifestyle is another aspect that an immigrant or a person from a minority culture learns quite quickly. Nakamura is addicted to a substance named 'Philopon.' He says to Fukuhara that Philopon "is an expression of Japanese spirit" (94) and that "only inferior races like the Chinese, Europeans, and Indians are addicted to opiates" (94). His conversation with Fukuhara means that although Nakamura is also addicted to opium which is not their lifestyle like people from other countries, he disagrees to have integrated. However, unconsciously Democratic pluralism has already taken place.

In *Gould's Book of Fish,* Rennie Conga is Italian by birth, and Gould is Australian, but they are fond of Americans who come to Australia for business. In return, the Americans are also fond of them. This liking for people from different cultures is the beginning of two cultures coming together with the people's will. (6), when the people from the superior culture misbehave with Gould, the latter presents the conversation as if he is one of them and they like him (45). Gould also works with a Dutchman, and there he learns the Dutch dance form to impress the masters (114). He now knows the dance form of his native land and the dance form of the culture of majority and dominance for which he works. This psyche of Gould shows that although the people of majority culture or the culture of natives do not want the person from a minority culture to mix up with them, the person of minority culture has a full right to keep both cultures together. Tracker Marks is a black "mainland native of Australia who once worked for Van Diemonian troopers tracking down the bushrangers." (219) Tracker Marks devises an accent blending two languages. Along with Tracker Marks, Capois Death joins Marks in the usage of this language. When the two converse on being alone, in a "jumpy argot of their own invention: a blend of English-influenced Creole and Aborigine-influenced English." (220) The blend of two languages, out of which one belongs to the savages, and the other belongs to the culture of the majority, shows the presence of Democratic pluralism in the society. Moreover, Tracker Marks, even though he is a back aborigine from the remotest areas of Australia, dresses "in the fashion of American whalers with whom he had once roamed the southern seas." (219) Apart from the dressing sense and language, Tracker Marks also learns the dance form of the "whitefellas" after he becomes expert in the emu dance and the kangaroo dance, which are the dance forms of his tribe. He now knows the dance forms of both cultures well, so much so that the members of his tribe cannot stop themselves from praising his "observation and stealthy imitation" when gathering around the fire (221).

Twopenny Sal is also one of the main characters of *Gould's Book of Fish*. She is a black aborigine who is a native of the remotest areas of Australia. She is initially forced to be a part of the dominant culture. The white people kidnap her only son and keep a condition in front of her. They say that if she wants her son back, she will have to come with the white society and be a slave to the people of the dominant and majority culture. She agrees to their condition and goes with them. However, the tragedy takes place when the whites kill her son even after agreeing to their conditions. Initially, she faced many issues assimilating, but slowly with time, after giving birth to the children of her owners, she wishes to learn the language of the dominant culture. She, thence, starts using both English words and the words from her mother tongue or the language of the minority culture. Not only language but the beliefs of the English people regarding their superiority also settle in her mind. She says "Numminer, Numminer" again and again. By this native word, she means that after the death of a black aborigine,

> "*... numminer was their word both for ghosts and white men, that they believed England was where their spirits went after death to be reborn as English men and women, that the white men were their ancestors returned. (221)*"

Mathinna is a black Aborigine character in *Wanting*, who catches the eyes of the wife of English governor Lady Jane who decides to take Mathinna into her society. She starts training Mathinna with the help of her maidservant Widow Munro. Mathinna has a dream to learn writing from the beginning of the novel and since her childhood, as she considers it magic that only whites know. This desire to learn to write makes it easier for her to adjust to English society. With time, she grows habitual to the lifestyle of the English society. The moment she enters society, it starts fascinating her, and it is "one of the overwhelming excitement" (113). The people in the Government house teach her the teachings of the English church, and back in her hometown, the Protector also used to teach all the blacks, the teachings of the English church in order to civilize them. When Mathinna lies alone in her expensive bed, she tries to unravel her many fathers. "...

God her Father, and Jesus his Son, who was also a sort of a father; there was the Protector, who had the Spirit of God the Father; and then there was Sir John, who was also her father, her new father— so many fathers" (113).

However, she writes the letter to her father that is Towterer. This introspection of Mathinna shows that she considers the people of the majority culture to be her father, the God and His Son as her fathers, and of course her father, Towterer. However, the chronology, with which she recalls all her fathers, shows that she has very well integrated with the English society and integration that is Democratic pluralism to be more specific as there is no pressure on Mathinna to believe what she believes. This integration is better seen when Mathinna goes to a party organized by the Governor and Lady Jane. There she comes all dressed up like an English woman. However, the song she chooses to sing is from her native land in Australia; she behaves with all the mannerisms of English society. However, the dance she chooses is the Emu dance that is the dance form of the aborigines of Australia (113).

Apart from the central characters, some minor characters show signs of integration without any pressure on them. Mr. Francis Lazaretto, Mathinna's tutor in the Government House, is from Sydney. However, in the company of Mathinna, he learns Mathinna's native language and the Aboriginal dance form that is Emu (128). Similarly, Lady Jane's maidservant Widow Munrow is a savage from some part of the world, but she trains Mathinna to be a part of the English society as she already is. She pretends to belong to an elite white class in front of Mathinna, and she learns all the mannerisms of English society, but when she is alone, she behaves naturally as a savage (122). Walter Talba Bruney, a black aborigine, whom the Protector educates, finds himself at ease with blacks and whites (218). Sir John, the Governor of English society, agrees to the ideas of his wife Lady Jane in civilizing the blacks and making them like the whites. However, as he spends more time with Mathinna, he starts feeling at his natural self in her company. He also learns Mathinna's ways from her (135).

The Sound of One Hand Clapping is a novel full of the characters' chaos, struggle, and adjustment in the majority's culture. The novel starts when the protagonist, Sonja Buloh, is just three years old. As the novel begins, her family has already left Slovenia and struggles to find their space in the foreign culture. The Beulah family comes across many people from various cultures and countries. Those who are not from the dominant culture are seen to be struggling from the beginning. The day Sonja turns sixteen in the year 1967, she prepares for the birthday party herself. She arranges things suiting to the taste of both Australians and Slovenians. This incident shows that Sonja and her family have gelled up with the Australians and have maintained their culture of origin's values and beliefs. Sonja "baked some cakes, not kids' cakes, but two lush chocolate cakes and a cheesecake of the type Australians liked. She bought salamis and cheeses and good bread..." (316). The list of items she prepared is a combination of the items liked by both Australians as well as Slovenians. Sonja's best friend Helvi is a native Australian and a white. Sonja finds her friend to be a bird from a foreign land which has landed in front of her as she hears her "English speech with its Finnish warble as a finch-like twitter" (75). Helvi has taken up the Finnish accent and added to her language that is English and this *integration* that she undertakes on her own will and wish without any pressure on her.

There are many instances where Bojan and his daughter Sonja converse in their native language that is Slovenian, but there are other instances where they talk only in English. There are also such instances where Bojan responds to a Slovenian question by Sonja with an answer in English. Bojan can be seen struggling to learn English but cannot succeed in being fluent in it. However, he continues using the English language that too in its broken form. "Though Bojan generally insisted that they speak English and not Slovene, he would, when feeling easy, tease her softly and play with words in his mother tongue." (213) Sonja befriends her American neighbor Moira Heaney and, while talking to her, takes up the American accent from the speech of Moira and in turn, teaches Slovene to the latter. The American accent that she borrows from her friend remains with Sonja throughout her life. Sonja then uses both Slovene and English with an American accent in them. Sonja takes up this American accent on her own, just like she chooses to learn and speak English instead of Slovene (160). When Maria, mother of the little protagonist Sonja, crosses the Australian canteen while leaving her home and the child behind, she hears the western music being played and the Australians enjoying the combination of two different cultures that is the traditional look the western music. This integration on the part of the Australians is self-wished and self-desired without any pressure on them (7).

The analysis of all the seven novels of Richard Flanagan above shows the trend and presence of Democratic pluralism amongst the people from minority cultures or the immigrants. In his research paper of 1974, Berry gave another type of integration: Parental integration or Inclusive segregation. In the words of Berry, parental integration is the pattern of a decision in which

> *"the dominant society requires the maintenance of ethnicity and positive intergroup relations. The ethnic individual is not entitled to take on either another set of cultural characteristics or to engage in negative relations with the dominant society. This pattern usually requires an efficient set of social-control agents (e.g. police or passes) for its enforcement. (19)"*

He gave another name to this type of integration: inclusive segregation. The individual does not choose whether to maintain both cultures, the dominant and the minority culture, equally. The people of the dominant culture demand that the minority culture and the culture of the majority be carried together by the immigrants or the people of minority culture whether the latter wish to do so or not

There are many incidents where the integration took place in the novels of Richard Flanagan but not by choice of the people of minority culture. They chose to be a part of the society of majority preserving their own culture, not by their choice, but due to the pressure of the powerful and dominant majority. After the Japanese power ends and the Prisoners of War are freed in *The Narrow Road to the Deep North,* the Japanese people, who earlier used to beat the prisoners and torture them, are now in America. Colonel Kota and Major Nakamura now live in America like the Americans and adopt their lifestyle while also maintaining their identities of being Japanese (320). This may not be the choice of both of them as they have been very adamant from the beginning and proud to tell and prove to everyone that they are Japanese. However, now, as they are in America and there are many Americans, they have to be one of them. Similarly, in *Wanting,* Robinson, or the Protector, is a white, assigned to civilizing the blacks while living with them. When Robinson goes to the living place of the black aborigines, the blacks are in the majority. Moreover, this is why Robinson joins the blacks in their singing and dancing, although he is embarrassed and does not want to join. (59) This is the power of the majority culture, whether it is black or white. The person from a minority culture is pressured either psychologically or socially to balance both cultures.

Tracker Marks in *Gould's Book of Fish* is a black aborigine residing in Australia, who is introduced to Robinson or the Protector by Towterer, the chief of black aborigines as a "flashman." (219) Tracker Marks once worked for the Van Diemonian troopers tracking down the bushrangers, but somehow he lands up joining Robinson in his mission to bring all the blacks from the wilderness and send them to the island made to keep them. He does not enjoy doing what he does but is not repelled by it. In his own words- "Robinson's party was a simple mob to travel with, but it was not his land through which he traveled, and though he was black, they were not his people." (220) In front of the whites, Tracker Marks behaves as if he is one of them and secretly maintains his culture and ideologies also, which are against those with whom and for whom he works. The nature of his work leads his dialect to be affected by it. He uses "dementung," which is a word of Van Diemonians for a dialect "that was part-blackfella, part-whitefellon." (325) He praises the white people, even though he does not like them much. The power and money, which seems to favor the whites, makes Marks turn to their support and pretend to be like them in their presence (221). Twopenny Sal is another prominent example of *integration* that is not wished by the migrant and is somehow forced by the dominant culture, white people in this case. The Whites kidnapped the son of Twopenny Sal and blackmailed her into coming along with them, and slowly with time, due to the power and dominance of the whites, she is forced to learn the language and lifestyle which never belonged to her. It further leads to Twopenny speaking her words for the ideologies given by the Whites.

In conclusion, it can be said that the traces of two strategies of the four-fold model of Acculturation by J. W. Berry can quite easily be seen in all the seven novels of Richard Flanagan. Berry gave two types of assimilation that are Melting Pot and Pressure cooker. Similarly, he divided the strategy of integration into Democratic pluralism and Parental integration. This division by Berry is based on the choice of immigrants whether or not to maintain their culture of origin and the native culture that is a culture of the majority. The characters from the texts fell in each category.

The present study has focused on understanding acculturation and its processes with the detailed analysis of two acculturation strategies out of four given by J.W. Berry. The concept of acculturation is a very general concept that was applied to culture specifically. The processes of acculturation are understood as given by J.W. Berry. Many models define the processes of acculturation, but the model given by Berry best suits the novels of Richard Flanagan. The strategies given by Berry cover all the aspects of acculturation as it explains four options or alternatives available to the immigrant or the person or people from minority groups based on the three questions- Is the culture of origin maintained? Is the culture of the majority of the native culture adopted? Does the immigrant make a choice?

The study has also explored the intricacies of acculturation in the fiction of Richard Flanagan' is also half achieved as all the seven novels of Richard Flanagan has been analyzed through the lens of assimilation and integration and the two types of each the two as discussed by Berry in 1974. The characters in the fiction of Richard Flanagan are vivacious. According to berry, there are "eight possible patterns of relations when three questions of psychological significance are posed, and when dichotomous answers are provided." (20) Out of these eight patterns, four patterns are applied to the texts in this chapter. It is found that there are many characters, major and minor, who fall in the category of the Melting pot, in which the immigrants or the people of minority culture choose themselves to assimilate, that is, leave their culture of origin and adopt the native culture or the culture of the majority. For instance, Bojan, father of the protagonist of *The Sound of One Hand Clapping*, when purchases a car of his own in a foreign land, very proudly says, "...it was a proof to both those in Slovenia and Australia that he had become what he had set out to be: Australian." (85)

Bojan, like many other characters, chooses to assimilate on their own will. Berry's second pattern of assimilation is Pressure cooker. The immigrants' choice to assimilate is not made; instead, it is forced on them by the people in the majority. For instance, in the novel *Wanting*, McMohan, a white, thrashes Mathinna and Walter Talba Bruney, black aborigines, to remember what the English church has taught him and not forget the fear of the whites' God. After assimilation, the following pattern Berry gave is Democratic integration. The choice to maintain the culture of origin and at the same time adopt the native culture is made by the immigrants. For instance, Maria Magdalena Svevo, born and brought up in Italy, buys Australian cigars as she starts loving them. After coming to Australia, she adopts the lifestyle of Australians and maintains many aspects of her original culture also. In the end, the fourth pattern given by Berry in 1974 is a subdivision of integration that is paternal integration or inclusive segregation. In this pattern, the decision to integrate is taken by the majority's culture because it is the need of the people of the majority culture. In the fiction of Richard Flanagan, there are a few characters that fall in this category. For instance, Tracker Marks, in *Gould's Book of Fish*, works for Robinson's party. Although he agrees that they are not his people, he still behaves like they want him to.

Assimilation and integration have a different effects on different characters based on the type of each of them given by Berry. For instance, by following the pattern of *melting pot,* the psychological condition of the individual characters is more peaceful as compared to the other type of assimilation that is *pressure cooker* in which the decision to leave the original culture and adopt the culture of majority is taken by the people of the dominant society. In the latter pattern, the individual faces the issues like depression. The social life of the individuals who adopt both the patterns of assimilation is peaceful and happy. Similarly, the psyche of the individual characters, which follow the pattern *of democratic pluralism,* have a peaceful mind as the decision of integrating is taken by the individuals themselves, as compared to those, who follow the other pattern of *integration,* that is *paternal integration,* in which the decision to carry both cultures together is forced upon them by the people of dominant society with the help of agents like the police. In the latter pattern, the individuals feel psychological pressure and, as a result, have a high risk of falling into a state of depression. The social life of characters in both types of integration is peaceful and happy. However, if the larger society is considered, the dominant culture expands as it adds new members. In the case of democratic pluralism and melting pot, the society grows peacefully. However, there is chaos to a certain extent in the case of pressure cooker and paternal integration. However, still, the dominant culture expands with the help of some forcing agencies.

State apparatus with its policies, police, judiciary and army and civil apparatus with aspects like customs, rituals etc. affect the process of assimilation and integration. Role of reason behind migration, condition at and of the motherland and future aspirations also affect the processes of assimilation and integration. Challenges for the first and second generations are different. Reaction towards the adoption or rejection of the majority culture also varies from generation to generation.

CHAPTER THREE

Segregation and Marginalization

In sociology, segregation is the practice or policy of creating separate facilities within the same society to use a minority group. It is a practice that compels racial groups to live apart from each other. These races are separate in terms of education, jobs, society, etc. According to dictionary.com, segregation is a practice that keeps one culture or group apart from the main body or the leading group. Racial segregation is also a similar term, but it limits to the separation of a particular race. It has nothing to do with a person or people of any culture. Segregation can be forced or self-imposed.

In his research paper published in 1974, J.W. Berry proposed eight patterns of answers to three questions relating to the decision regarding maintenance of relations between the majority culture and the culture of origin. He talked about his four-fold model of acculturation earlier also but discussed it in detail and with much clarity on the idea of acculturation in the paper of 1974. He suggested there are two types of segregation-rejection or self-segregation and exclusive segregation. In both types, the immigrant or the people from minority culture retain their culture of origin and do not maintain positive relations with the dominant culture. The only difference is that in the former, the people of minority cultures make a choice; whereas in the latter, the decision is imposed by the dominant culture forcefully. In Berry's own words, rejection or self-segregation is the decision pattern in which "...the ethnic group(s) affirm their culture and identity but deny the usefulness of positive intergroup relations. Among highly acculturated ethnic groups, this pattern is often referred to as "reaffirmation"..." (19)

He gives examples of the "Red or Black Power Movements in America, Celtic Nationalism in Europe and Negritude in Africa" (19) for the pattern of rejection. The second type of segregation, according to Berry, is exclusive segregation, which was prevalent a few decades ago when it was possible for the dominant culture to forcefully exclude the minority cultural groups from participating in the significant happenings or activities of the majority culture legally and economically (19). Berry later states that these days, the adoption of democratic values and a "recognition of the economic value of the ethnic groups has lessened the frequency of this pattern." (19)

According to britannica.com, segregation is made up of two dimensions-vertical segregation and horizontal segregation. Also, it can be extreme segregationist policies due to which the oppressed or the people of a minority culture are denied any civil or political rights. This kind of segregation has been practiced since very long back in history which can be seen through the sufferings of women, homosexuals, members of the caste, various religious groups. There have been various social reform movements also that have been ignited by the continuous brutal oppression. Another type of segregation can be the one that is self-imposed or voluntary. In this type of segregation, minority cultures think that the culture can be preserved better if they separate themselves from the mainstream culture. They only mix up with the people of the dominant culture geographically or residentially.

In a YouTube lecture on the channel 'Vidya-mitra,' the speaker explains the four-fold model given by Berry. In the process, explaining the concept of separation, she says, "it takes place when an individual strongly tries to hold on to his/her culture of origin and refuses to take the initiative to interact with the people of the other or the new culture..." and later gives an example of an American employee sent to Japan to take charge of the company officials who choose to cling on to his American attitude and ways of getting work done. The term separation has different meanings when it is applied in other contexts. For example, in 1970, J.W. Berry used the term separation for the process of acculturation in ethnocultural groups, in which one clings to their cultural values and denies the adoption of the majority culture. But later in the year 1974, he divided each of the acculturation processes or his four-fold model into two. While talking about the process of separation, he used the term segregation. In 2001, Berry spoke about the strategies or processes of acculturation in a larger society mentioning segregation again.

When the immigrants or the people from minority cultures adopt either marginalization or separation, it leads to the state known as "acculturative stress," proposed by Berry in his research paper published in 1970. Oberg presented a similar concept in the year 1960 that is "culture shock." The meaning conveyed by both the terms is almost the same as both deal with the psychological dealing of the intercultural interaction and the situations that result from it. But, out of these two terms, the former proposed by Berry is preferred for two reasons. One, the term "shock" has pathological overtones.

In contrast, "stress" has a theoretical basis for studies on how people deal with stressors. This difference is because the stress emerges from the interaction between two cultures and, therefore, "acculturative" and not one culture. Before Berry's theory came on screen, people and theorists used to think that when two cultures interact, this process is very smooth, and people involved in acculturation very quickly adopt each others' culture. But Berry's concept of "acculturative stress" has completely changed the scenario, as he believed that every individual reacts to the acculturation process differently.

The fourth strategy or the process of acculturation, according to J.W. Berry, is marginalization. But later, in 2001, when applying his four-fold acculturative model to a larger society, Berry renamed it exclusion. According to Berry, marginalization has two types of possibilities- marginality and deculturation based on the answers to the three questions on which he based his four-fold model: Is the original identity of the immigrants or the people from minority culture retained? Are the relations with the majority culture positive? And finally, is it the people of minority culture's choice to make decisions, or is it forced? In the case of marginality, the answer to the first two questions is "yes," but the answer to the third question is "no." And in the case of deculturation, the answer to all three questions is "no." In the words of Berry, in the pattern of marginality,

> "*...ethnic groups, apparently without pressure, occupy a position between two cultural systems, belonging to neither and having few positive intergroup contacts. Examples of this pattern are Part-Aborigines in Australia, Metis in Canada, and Anglo-Indians in India; however many are developing a new culture and, if successful, may move into patterns one or three (Integration or Rejection).* (20)"

In this pattern, the people of a minority group or the immigrants do not belong to one particular group and lie somewhere between both the groups. Still, there are positive contacts and there is a hope that the relations can one day become better. There is a sense of peace in the immigrants' lives compared to when they follow this pattern of marginalization that is deculturation. According to Berry, the pattern of deculturation is very damaging as there is no hope left in the people of minority culture and suggests that the term is not appropriate as "apathy" and "withdrawal" become their "dominant feature." He means that although the people have their own "way of life" and how they deal with the situations, the pattern is still very "unsupportive." He terms it as a "culture of poverty." (20)

Rahul Sharma, in his YouTube lecture "marginalization," defines the marginal group of people as "the people who feel ignorant in a particular society." Similarly, the speaker in a YouTube lecture on "Vidya-mitra" defines marginal as "considered to be the oppressed and exploited sections of the society" and further suggests that generally, this term is considered to be an antonym of the mainstream. In his 1998 book *Constructing Co-Cultural Theory*, Mark Orbe proposed a new word for marginalized the co-culture group. He based his theory on the "muted group theory," as suggested by Edwin Ardener and Shirley Ardener in the mid-1970s. The "muted group theory" focuses on how the marginalized group is muted and how language excludes them from the mainstream. According to this theory, the dominant culture formulates the language system, vocabulary, and social norms, which are to be followed by the marginalized group of people. As a result, they are expected to express themselves in a language that is not theirs and need to learn before speaking. Eventually, these expectations and events make them a muted group as they fail to express themselves in the dominant language. It was mainly developed for studying marginalized women that means it was supposed to be a feminist theory. Still, it can be applied to other silenced groups in society.

Mark Orbe gave twenty-six different types of ways that the "underrepresented" groups can undertake to interact with the dominant group. He presented this list after he found out that a white European studied the communication process of Africans in America and concluded that irrespective of age, sex, gender, class, etc., all African-Americans interact with the dominant group in the same way. Orbe gave the "co-culture communication theory" and defined it as "communication between dominant and non-dominant group members." (51) According to him, there are three significant outcomes of this communicative process- assimilation, accommodation, and separation. There is a possibility of three communication approaches in each of these three- non-assertive, assertive, and aggressive.

According to freedictionary.com, marginalization is "the process in which individuals or entire communities of people are systematically blocked from (or denied full access to) various rights, opportunities and resources that are normally available to members of a different group (e.g., housing, employment, healthcare, civic engagement, democratic participation, and due process)." Berry, in his 1997 paper Immigration, Acculturation, and Adaptation, considers it to be a fact that the state of marginalization is a result of failed trials and that the "...rather they usually become marginalized as a result of attempts at forced assimilation (Pressure Cooker) combined with forced exclusion (Segregation)." (10)

According to Berry, in recent studies, it has been found that in societies with a melting pot nature, integration strategy remained the most adaptive and marginalization the least. Berry, in 2006, developed a scale- "acculturation attitudes" that posed four different statements to measure which strategy out of four is most preferred and which one least. In the statement about marginalization, it was stated- "I don't want to attend either [national] or [ethnic] social activities." (309)

These two strategies or the processes: segregation and marginalization negatively affect society and the individual struggling to acculturate. But there can be various outcomes of both of them based on the division given by Berry of each of them. The novels of Richard Flanagan will hence be analyzed thoroughly from the lens of these two folds out of the four-fold model of acculturation. The characters of the books and the situations will be categorized based on the sub-divisions of each of them.

Berry gave two subdivisions ofsegregation: self-segregation, which is also known as rejection, and 'exclusive segregation.' The significant difference between the two is that in the former, the immigrants or the people from minority groups segregate themselves as in, there is no pressure on them, but they decide to stick to the culture of origin and reject the idea of accepting or adopting the native culture or the culture of the majority. In the latter, the dominant group is pressured to decide that the minority culture would not be accepted in the majority culture and keep their culture with them. As per this theory, there are various instances where segregation could be seen in the fiction of Richard Flanagan.

As far as self-segregation or rejection is concerned, the black aborigines in the novel *First Person* do not want the white settlers to intrude or interfere in their cultural matters. They are happy to maintain their own culture and want the whites to be away from their women. There is an incident when Kif, the protagonist, and his friend Ray go to a place that belongs to the black aborigines in search of black women to satisfy their lust. The black men start coming closure to them in rage, in a mood to kill both of them, as noticed by Kif when he says- "I don't think they like us being with their women... The circle began tightening around us in what felt an inexorable noose." (57)

The black men and the two girls, who are known by the color of their dresses as Pink and Purple, show that they do not want any sort of interference in their cultures. The girls observed that Kif and Ray are not worth mixing up they segregate themselves abusing the Tasmanians as both the boys are from Tasmania by birth. Pink is from Norway, and after realizing that these Tasmanians are not trustworthy, she says, "Shit-eating two-head Tasmanians." (133) Both of these instances show that people choose to segregate themselves on their own will deciding to reject the dominant culture and retain their own culture of origin. These choices can be made under different circumstances.

Maria Magdalena Svevo is an essential character in the life of Aljaz, the protagonist of *Death of a River Guide*. She helps Aljaz's mother in childbirth when Aljaz is born. She is from Trieste, Italy, by birth. She migrates to Australia, but some habits show that she rejects to change according to the dominant culture. Like the attire she wears at the funeral of Aljaz's mama is in the fashion in Trieste, which is the culture of origin and not in style in Tasmania. Apart from dressing sense, language is another significant element that shows that although she is in Australia, she still belongs to Trieste's culture of origin. She is in the habit of saying "Madonna Santa" again and again. It is an Italian word that means "Good Heavens." She says in a Triestino accent, "Vanity of vanities, saith the preacher. All is vanity. One generation passeth away, and another generation cometh: but the earth abideth forever." (8)

Rose, Harry's mother, is from Richmond and is proud of her culture of origin as she proudly says about her home that it is, "... a place where people knew their place and where, she said, her family was much respected because her mother was a woman of some culture..." (51) She marries Boy, Harry's father, from Australia, but she never mixesin the majority culture in Australia but chooses to retain her own culture. Although it had adverse effects on her psychological and married life, this is the option she chooses by her own will. Sonja, Harry's wife, and Aljaz's mother, moves to Australia with her husband and a three-year-old child, Aljaz. Initially, she adopts the Australian culture but slowly segregates herself and rejects the majority culture, keeping the culture of origin. Sonja closes her mind to the present culture as she keeps on searching for something ancient that she can relate to her past life in her country, although the city in Australia is not very old. With time, Sonja grows old, but a particular thing about her makes her growing old very unique. "She became an old European mama" (147) as she chooses to keep the European culture with her and reject the culture of the majority of the culture of her husband. However, the narrator Aljaz tells us that the marriage of Harry and Sonja is not a failure because Sonja rejects the culture, but she loves her husband very much. Even after marriage, as is the tradition worldwide, Sonja plans to keep her family's surname with her name that is Cosini. Sonja proves to be a strong and determined lady as she takes independent steps in life going against all the social conventions. She meets Harry in Trieste, Italy, and conceives Aljaz before marriage. Unfortunately, Harry is imprisoned, and after he comes out of jail, she decides not to marry him but to give birth to Aljaz and live with Harry without marriage. But because Harry broke her trust once, she decides that she will keep her family's surname and even Aljaz also keeps the surname of his mother, Cosini. With the same determination and assertive attitude, she decides to maintain her culture of origin, and till the day she dies, she remains a European and never becomes an Australian.

Adie is Aljaz's friend and is as black as the latter. They are school friends, but the difference between them is that Adie is proud of his culture of origin and rejects to mix with the majority's culture. Adie joins Aljaz in his fight as the latter struggles to prove that the blacks need to be accepted as they are. Still, as his mission could not be accomplished, Adie leaves the place as his father gets transferred to the north but leaves with a sense of pride that he still maintains his original identity. A white man sits with four black ladies at the seashore towards the end of the novel. They discuss religion, but this discussion is one-sided as the dominant white culture dominates the debate. He gets violent when he realizes that his belief in the dominant culture is not being respected. He goes to the extent of slapping the women and makes them agree that he is superior to them. Although in this four-fold model of *acculturation*, the people of minority groups segregate themselves, rejecting the majority's culture, it can also be applied to the dominant culture when the people of the dominant culture are in the native areas of the culture of the minority. Sitting with four black ladies, the white man segregates himself, rejecting the non-dominant culture and calling that culture inferior. He says it very proudly while slapping the black lady who speaks against his religion the most, "Learn this and learn it well... I was made in the image of our Lord... White... White... And God gave me dominion over all his creatures... Including you... Including you." (313) Harry, the father of the protagonist Aljaz, has an aunt named Auntie Ellie. She is black, but she feels attached and emotional to the people and her origin culture and shows the same attachment when she dies. People say that when a person dies, s/he never lies. When she lies dying, Auntie Ellie says that her people call her the people who have already died and ask Harry not to cry for her (208). Throughout her life, she struggles to be accepted by the whites in the dominant society, pretends to belong to a wealthy white elite class, and avoids saying that she is black. But later in her life, she accepts the truth and calls the blacks her people, which is a big deal for a lady like her. She rejects the idea of belonging to the dominant white culture and decides to maintain her culture of origin.

One day, when Aljaz visits a bar, where Shag and his band sing live songs, the former feels the pain in the latter's song. Shag's sister has left the country believing that she will go away from this place. She feels ashamed to be associated with the culture of origin and assimilates into the new and the dominant culture. Shag, her brother, on the other hand, feel attached and proud of his culture of origin and decides not to accept the culture of dominance and maintain his own culture by his own will. Although he chooses to stay home in the home country, keeping the home culture, he feels the pain at the loss of his sister. This pain is felt by Aljaz in the former's song 'If you leave, you can never be free' (257), suggesting the opinion of Shag about being stuck to one's root culture to be the true definition of freedom and independence and that if one assimilates in the dominant culture leaving the root culture behind, they can never be independent. Similarly, Aljaz, who is an Australian, is proud of his own culture and country. Although he regularly contacts many people of the dominant culture, he never leaves his culture of origin. He maintains loyalty and attachment to his culture. His love for his own country and hatred for the dominant culture of white people is seen in his thoughts as he discusses them repeatedly in the novel. He wonders once, on his own,

> *"... the English had an idea that a single man could own land for his advancement? ... Was it this: the white imagining, which grappled with and overwhelmed the black knowledge by claiming as its own the land that lay at the root of the black knowledge?... Or was it something the convicts and blackfellas shared that divided them yet might one day bring them all together? (258)"*

Aljaz comes to understand the strategies behind all the actions of the white people to expand their territories and their culture so that they can maintain their dominance and rule the world in a monopoly, and this is why he rejects the alliance with the dominant culture very strongly and keeps his relation with the root culture. He loves the customs, traditions, values, beliefs, etc., that are associated with his culture. Moreover, he feels proud to be an Australian. These reasons are enough for a person to self-segregate himself, rejecting the dominant culture and maintaining the culture of origin.

In *The Unknown Terrorist*, the Doll, the novel's protagonist, is always eager to look white and wants to be seen and accepted as belonging to an elite white class. She runs after brands throughout her life to be counted among the affluent white- dominant society. There comes a day when she realizes that no matter how hard she has been trying to leave her past and her culture of origin, but she has never been able to get rid of it. She always sticks to the culture of origin. Similarly, a cab driver is Vietnamese by birth, and due to his job as a taxi driver in Australia, he has to live there. But he is not very happy with his life there as he says that they are not allowed to do what they want to do, they can't even play music of their choice in their cabs in Australia due to the rules and regulations there.

The novel *The Narrow Road to the Deep North* is the perfect example of a story full of instances where so many cultures live in the same place but are always different. No one mixes. The segregation there is on both cultures, may it be the dominant one or the non-dominant one. The novel is about the Japanese target of building a railway line for which various POWs, Prisoners of War, are used to achieve it. The people who are prisoners in Japan and are working for them are from different countries. Some are from south India; some are from Korea, majority of them are from Australia. These people maintain their original culture with pride even though they are tortured and ill-treated because they are not Japanese. There comes a time in Australia when people starve due to poverty and lack of food. But even in such conditions, the people of Australia "tried to hold together with their Australian dryness and their Australian curses, their Australian memories and their Australian mate ship." (50) The people of Australia try their best to stick to their culture of origin till their last breath as they keep on rejecting the culture of the majority which was also the dominant culture. In Japan, where there are so many cultures living under the same roof and working for the dominant culture, the Japanese people are proud of their culture; the Japanese officers sit till late in the nights and tell each other the stories of Japanese honor and of the legends that make them feel proud of their culture. They contact thousands of people from different cultures daily, but their pride in their own culture becomes stronger and stronger with every meeting. This sense of pride goes to the extent that the two Japanese officers talk openly about their superiority and the inferiority of the other culture. Colonel Kota says to Nakamura- "It is not just about the railway, though the railway must be built. Or even the war, though the war must be won. It is about the Europeans learning that they are not the superior race, Nakamura said. And us learning that we are, Colonel Kota said." (125)

The hatred for other cultures is not only in the dominant culture but also in the non-dominant culture. It is usually believed that the non-dominant group has the maximum chances to have a desire to be like the people of the majority group as they wish to be treated well. But this is not the case here in this novel. The people who belong to the inferior culture or the non-dominant culture hate the people of the dominant culture all the way more. This hatred can be seen in Jack Rainbow when he shows his anger for a Japanese guard. Darky Gardiner and Jack Rainbow are in conversation, and there the latter shows his hatred for the people of the dominant culture. He says, "... you know what? If I had a chance I'd split him from eye to arsehole with a blunt razor blade." (42)

Dorrigo, the protagonist of the novel, has an uncle named Uncle Keith. The latter has complete knowledge about the culture of America and Russia. He rejects the culture of both the countries but leaves them with his own will and maintains his own culture, considering them superior to the rest of the cultures. In Japan, all the POWs live in a chaotic and disturbing place where they are prone to so many diseases bred due to the unhygienic conditions in the POW camps. In the novel, people from different cultural backgrounds live under the same roof carrying all the hatred for the cultures in their hearts. Rooster MacNeice, thinking that Jimmy Bigelow is a Victorian, starts criticizing the Tasmanians who live in the same room, saying that if the latter wants to prevent his intellect from stagnating, he needs to stay away from "convict-bred, card playing, football-worshipping, horseracing-addicted Tasmanians" (192). This dialogue shows his rejection for not only the dominant culture but also for other cultures he stays with. He considers his own culture to be best and therefore sticks to it with his own will. He misses his home culture as he finds it difficult to adjust to the "alien" and "unwelcoming" world around him (208), not because people are not good, this is because he doesn't want to leave his culture and adopt any feature of the other culture. Dorrigo, the novel's protagonist, is an Australian and works as a doctor for the POWs. He hates the Japanese in the majority and calls them "clamps" and "fucking yellow bastards." (275) He maintains his culture of origin throughout the novel without any sort of internal or external pressure.

Towards the end of the novel, the scenario changes completely. The people who were dominant in the beginning have no more dominance by the end. Major Nakamura, who once used to be an officer in Japanese rule, is now in America as all those who used to be dominant in the beginning are now at the disposal of the Australian law and order. To save his life, Nakamura migrates to America and starts working there. In America, American culture is the dominant culture, and the Japanese culture, to which Nakamura belongs, is a non-dominant one. Although he belongs to the minority culture, he is still not ready to put his culture at stake. He works for the Americans, lives amongst the people of the dominant class but is still proudly Japanese. He even scolds a prostitute once, asking her how she manages to spend the night with an American. This is again an example of solid self-segregation or rejection where the Americans are the ones who will decide the lifestyle of Nakamura. However, still, he rejects adopting their culture. Similarly, there is a minor character named Tiny, a white man under the rule of the dominant Japanese. These people, who are taken as the prisoners of war, are assigned to make a very long railway track for the Japanese to expand their territory and power. Tiny finishes his tasks before the given time and considers it his victory over the Japanese captors. On completing his studies earlier than everyone else, he proudly explains his side, saying, "Show them, little yellow bastards, what a white man is." (275)

Like the novel *The Narrow Road to the Deep North*, *Wanting* also has many instances in which some major and minor characters willingly maintain the culture of origin and reject the culture of dominance or majority. The novel *Wanting* is a brilliant portrayal of the effects of one dominant and one non-dominant culture coming in contact. The English rule the Australian aborigines in the story, and the latter want to civilize the former to make them like them. Mathinna, the protagonist of the novel, is a little black girl who attracts the attention of everyone as she seems to be different from other kids of her culture. She loves a red dress that she wears all the time. The governor of the white society Mr. John and his wife, Lady Jane, has a unique role in molding the track of the life of the little black girl Mathinna. Robinson is a white man who is assigned a task to civilize the black Australian aborigines. He makes many efforts to civilize them, but Mathinna uses her native language to talk even after all his efforts. He often asks her not to use the savage language and be like the white people to lead a better life. She says the word "Rowra" for "Devil" repeatedly even after his repeated warnings (10). Robinson christens her name as Leda because he does not want her to be associated with anything related to her root culture, but his efforts go in vain.

Lady Jane takes Mathinna with her as she is very impressed by her looks and her charming style of talking and behaving. She wants her to assimilate with the white culture so that the dominant white culture could expand its territory. She tries her best to civilize the black girl, but when she finds that there is no use in making any effort, as Mathinna cannot leave her culture of origin, she says, "She is exasperation" as "... the black child would not become white" (174). The course of her life has many ups and downs as she is sent to an English orphanage after Mr. John and Lady Jane find out that she can't be civilized and after Mathinna meets the people of her own culture on coming out of the orphanage, she sits with her black aborigine friend Walter Talba Bruney. She questions the authenticity of the religion and faith of the whites after realizing that her culture is the best and decides to reject the dominant culture. Her eyes open up, and hence she says,

> *"... There was no light at the end, no redemption, no justice. God, heaven whitefella talk- all tricks of the Devil. There was no black dreaming, no white heaven, only that bugger, the Devil, buggering everything. (220)"*

Mathinna and Walter Talba Bruney, the two friends, decide that "They would live on their wheat and potatoes, their muttonbirds and eggs and sheep. They did not need whitefellas ruling them." (219) Not only these two black Australian aborigines, but the other black people also revolt in their way to show their rejection of the dominant culture and decision to maintain their culture of origin. The tame blacks, who are at the disposal of the protector that is Robinson, run away with other black aborigines and tell them to kill the white man or kill themselves. They "had shot stock-keepers, looted shepherds' huts, burnt houses, killed two whalers" (217). The blacks want to be left alone with their culture and traditions of origin. At the beginning of the novel, we are told that Robinson, who is assigned the task of civilizing the black Australian aborigines, makes many arrangements for the savages to make them habitual to the lifestyle and the habits of the people of the dominant culture. He makes separate houses for them, teaches them the language of the dominant white culture, and even puts them on a diet taken by the white people so that they depend entirely on the white culture for their survival. Robinson notes that

> "... *the more they died, the more they wanted to cast off their English clothes and stop eating their English food, and move out of their English homes, which they said were filled with the Devil, and return to the pleasures of the hunt of a day and the open fire of a night. (2)*"

This observation of Robinson can be seen at two levels- one, the blacks realize that their culture is best and hence want to segregate themselves, rejecting the luxurious lifestyle of the dominant white culture; second, the repeated use of the word "their" by Robinson shows that the latter believe that the blacks have already assimilated with the lifestyle and culture of the whites. Now they leave their new and better culture to return to the savage culture of origin full of barbarism. The blacks return to their culture of birth, and when Robinson comes to meet them, they make him come down to their culture. They do not trust him for two reasons: he is white, and second, he carries guns with him. They do not show that they do not trust him, but they pretend to be as if they have mixed up with him. The black aborigines, along with those who run from Robinson's marked territory of the target audience, that is to be civilized or from his civilization camp, make him dance naked with them in their original cultural traditions and style. They celebrate the night in their customary ways and blacken Robinson's white face and make him strip down as if to make him acceptable (59). Early next morning, after waking up, Robinson finds that Towterer (the leader of the blacks) and all the black aborigines have left the place when Robinson was asleep. They pretend to be with Robinson to prevent the latter from taking them away and forcing them to assimilate. They choose to maintain their culture of origin with their own will and betray Robinson, who thinks he has successfully befooled them. Towterer, the chief of the blacks, is the one who never leaves the rituals and traditions of his culture of origin. When his wife dies, Robinson wants him to bury his wife with the English customs, but he cremates his wife in how his own culture taught him.

The novel *The Sound of One Hand Clapping* deals with segregation at different levels, for instance, language, lifestyle, dressing, etc. There is a constant struggle of minority cultures to prevent their culture of origin from vanishing. They choose to keep their culture and reject the dominant culture without any pressure. They wage war against the white people trying to rule them. The minority cultures hear so many legends and about a night "of their fierce war against the invading whitefellas." (21) The most number instances are from the aspect of language, which shows that people of minority cultures choose to speak their language and reject the language spoken by the people of majority. Maria Buloh, the mother of the three-year-old protagonist, uses her native Slovenian tongue to soothe her little daughter, saying "Aja, aja" (2) so many times. Maria sings a lullaby to her infant daughter in her native tongue that she remembers her mother singing to her (261). This lullaby makes her old memories revive and connect her back to her culture of origin in an alien world of Australians. The family of Sonja moves from Slovenia to Australia in search of work and a better living standard. But her mother, Maria, still speaks her native tongue.

This case is not with Maria alone; the other people who migrate from other countries to the Australian culture choose their language over the dominant Australian. The little girl, Sonja, as her mother, speaks Slovenian pleading with the earth, saying, "Ni, Artie, ni, ni, ni..." (14), in which "Artie" means father. One day while playing, Sonja says, "Turksa kava for artie— turks kava for Mama— turksa kava for Sonja." (31) One day, when Sonja turns 15, her father Bojan beats her up, and she begs in front of him asking him not to beat her in her native tongue. She says, "Ni, Artie, ni, ni, ni..." (272). When Sonja returns to her home in the year 1990, she feels the essence of her home and calls it a "Doma," her father smiles and repeats the word of the native tongue. This exchange of a single word of the language of their culture of origin gives both of them immense pleasure and a sense of belonging in an alien world. Bojan wants his daughter to learn English as he knows that she will need this foreign language to secure a better future, but if it comes to him, he hates the language of the dominant class and has a never-ending love for his native language.

Apart from language, lifestyle is another aspect that needs some attention. Bojan is always attracted to the Australian culture as it is dominant and has power. But later in his life, he willingly rejects the dominant lifestyle and turns to his native Slovenian lifestyle. Bojan and Sonja eat in "Slovenian fashion from the pan, bursting the yolks and scooping up bits of egg, sausage and tomato all together on a single piece of broken bread, laughing and smiling as they did so…" (155) Bojan dislikes the Australian culture of a single bed system that is a single bed for a single person, considers it "odd and destructive" (217), and admires the Slovenian concept. Some more habits of Bojan show his link to the culture of origin and hatred for the majority's culture. Even Sonja dresses herself for occasions that she used to see in Europe when she was a child. She associates herself with the culture of origin and, staying in Australia, rejects the way of dressing that is prevalent here.

Gould's Book of Fish is another excellent example of characters that strongly reject the majority culture and stick to their home culture of non-dominant culture. Twopenny Sal is a black Australian aborigine who has kids and is leading a happy life. However, she catches the eye of a few men of the dominant white society. These men force her to come to their society and be their slave by abducting her son, whom she loves the most. She goes with them without her will on one condition: they will leave her son if she comes with them. But everything goes wrong, and they kill the black child. In the rage of her son's death and forcing Twopenny to leave her culture and adopt the dominant culture, the latter takes revenge from the whites by killing the children of these white men she gives birth to (218). Twopenny practices the rituals and traditions of her culture of origin. Later in life, she remains in Van Diemen's Land, her native country, and does not change her orientation from culture of origin to the culture of majority when all the people around her were mixing with the dominant culture leaving their culture of origin behind (147). She abandons a few things that she is forced to adopt when she lives with the white men in the dominant society.

"*She had abandoned her European clothes and apart from a red ochre smeared necklace... she wore nothing other than red ochre smeared on her face and through her public hair, the latter looking like rusty iron shavings attracted by the magnet of her pudenda. Her hair had been remade with a thick pomade of red ochre and grease, fashioned into overlapping scales like those of a fish. The children were similarly naked and similarly decorated. (328)"*

This description of the looks of Twopenny Sal indicates that she has embraced her culture of origin and rejected the culture of the majority of the dominant culture by her own will. It is common to note that the dominant society wants the non-dominant community to leave the culture of origin and become their slaves by accepting the inferiority. The Portuguese traders come and wish to do business in Australia, the black aborigines' land. In return for the land the former need, they offer many gifts as baits to the aborigines, but the latter revolt against the idea of snatching their land by rejecting the gifts. They do so to prevent their culture, which the Portuguese businessmen want to take away in the name of trading (242). Rolo Palma is a Vlech but lands in England amid English people and makes many friends from England. He is afraid of losing the culture of origin and hence decides to speak to angels rather than talking to English people and mixing up with them. This effort by Rolo shows his will to preserve his culture of origin and reject the culture of the majority (162). Similarly, Gould, the protagonist of the novel, chooses a unique way to show the struggle to preserve and protect the link to his own culture of origin. He shows this struggle through painting (92) segregation, as has been said earlier, cannot be limited to the minority culture. The people of majority culture decide to stick to the culture of origin and not to adopt the features of other minority cultures living around them. The commandant in the novel tries to make a second Europe on Sarah Island by making the people of minority cultures adopt his culture of origin, which he considers superior (157). All the instances mentioned above are of the process of segregation or separation. The choice to keep one's culture of origin and reject the majority's culture is taken by the people themselves without any pressure. But another type of segregation, as given by Berry, is exclusive segregation in which the decision to maintain one's culture of origin is not taken by the people of minority culture but is forced upon them by the people of majority culture as it is their wish to keep the people of minority culture separate from the mainstream and not to involve them in their superior civilization. However, there are not many instances of this type of segregation due to the democratic nature of the system in many countries.

In the novel *Death of the River Guide*, the black aborigines who desire to lead a better life, and the white prisoners, who are considered to be below the black aborigines who used to leave themselves at the will of the white people, dare to leave the country and move to the country of the white people. But "the prudish people of the colony of Victoria passed a law forbidding them to emigrate to that land" (258). The people of the dominant culture do not allow other cultures to mix up with them, and they force them to maintain the culture of origin. The same thing happens with Adie, a school friend of the protagonist Aljaz. Adie is "as black as Aljaz," and he seems to be "in a state of a permanent war with all the other school kids." (90) The other students force Adie and Aljaz to limit themselves to their own culture and keep this in mind that they are black and hence different and not acceptable. Both the boys are forced by the students of the culture of the majority to maintain their culture of origin. All of the classmates Aljaz are once invited to Phil Hodge's tenth birthday party except Aljaz. Phil's younger brother says, "But not you, Cosini... We don't have wogs... Especially not snotty red-headed wogs." (89) Even the teacher of Aljaz says, "those migrants' hygene" (89). When a teacher thinks like this about the migrants, what can be expected from her to teach students of the majority or dominant culture?

In *Narrow Road to the Deep North*, the dominant Japanese culture takes the people of other cultures as prisoners of war. The people of minority cultures from various countries work for the Japanese without their will. They are mistreated by the Japanese. Even if they want to, the people cannot love the dominant culture because of the way they are treated. The question of making a shift to the dominant culture leaving the non-dominant culture is far off. The non-Japanese people are beaten up by the officers of Japan just because they belong to the dominant culture. The people in authority beat up the non-Japanese in mud surrounded by the people of culture to which the person being beaten belongs. They are very helpless as they

> *"... wanted to rush the guards, seize the Goanna and the two others, beat them senseless, smash their skulls in until watery grey matter dribbled out, tie them to a tree and run their bayonets in and out of their guts... The prisoners thought that and then they thought that they cannot think that. (286)"*

Similarly, the Australian natives, in the novel *The Sound of One Hand Clapping,* behave coarsely with the non-Australians calling them "wogs" and making them live in entirely separate apartments they have names as "wog apartments." (146). Again, this sort of behavior of the dominant culture with the non-dominant cultures shows the helplessness of the people belonging to the minority culture that they do not want to be what they are but are forced by the dominant culture to maintain the culture of origin.

In his research paper published in 1974, Berry proposed four pillars or strategies of acculturation, namely assimilation, integration, separation, and marginalization. Marginalization, like the other three, has two types- marginality and deculturation. Marginalization is a process in which the people from the minority culture leave both the cultures and stay alienated. The difference between the two is that in marginality, the people of minority culture leave their culture of origin and the culture of the majority of the native culture by their own will. There is no internal or external pressure on them. They keep themselves away from participation in any sort of social involvement of both cultures. This situation leads to many side effects, but the person or people involved are happy in their zones because it is their choice. But in deculturation, the people of native culture or the culture of majority force the people of minority culture to remain outside their cultural events or the events of the dominant society. This process of marginalization is rarely found because maximum governments are democratic, and democracy doesn't allow anyone to dominate or rule the other. So there are no forced decisions to outcast the minority cultures seen these days.

In the novels of Richard Flanagan, there are many instances of marginality, but there are only a few cases of deculturation seen. The characters in *Wanting* show the feature of withdrawal from both cultures without any sort of pressure on them. Mathinna is the little protagonist of the novel who is taken by the white governor Mr. John and his wife Lady Jane to their society to civilize her and make her like white. Initially, Mathinna likes the white culture because she thinks white culture is superior and that writing is magic known only by white people. However, although she is taken to live with the white people and gives her best, she finds her culture of origin hinders her from becoming entirely like a white. Then there comes a situation when she accepts that she behaves weirdly: no culture- neither the aborigine culture nor the white culture.

*"Occasionally the spindly girl said something because she had to,
and, floating above, she could understand that she spoke in a manner
that was neither white not black, but in a strange way with strange
words that made no sense to anyone. Who was this girl? Why did she
talk this way, why this strange wavering voice? (213)"*

The explanation to these questions gives all the answers to prove that the
girl withdraws from both the cultures with her wish and that there is no
societal pressure on her. Nothing matters to her now as she says, "Kill me
too, then" (214). Towards the end of the novel, some people see Mathinna
working at a place well known for prostitution. They find it challenging
to figure out why she behaves in the way she does. She cuts herself from
everyone and everything. One of them remarks, "It was hard to know
whether her seeming acceptance was submission or simple-mindedness or
the most profound revolt, a contempt greater than any visited or her by pox-
raddled redcoats, shepherds or ticket-of-leave men." (227) People taunt her.
The people of both the cultures that are the culture of Mathinna's origin
and the dominant culture say that she has become "just another black ape"
(229) as they find her alienated and depressed and behaving in a particular
way that belongs to no specific culture. But that alienation is self-developed
by Mathinna. Moreover, Mathinna has no definite opinion on the aspect
of God as the white people taught her about Jesus. Then she forgets about
the rituals and beliefs of her culture of origin. But when she is rejected
by the people of the dominant society, after finding out that she cannot
be tamed the way they want her to be, she starts disbelieving the God of
the dominant culture also (243). Similarly, Walter Talba Bruney, a black
friend of Mathinna, is lost between the concepts of God, Jesus, savages, and
civilization. This confusion leads to the fact that the arbitrary concepts of
both cultures are not understandable to him now after he has experienced
the life of people of both cultures (245).

The novel *The Narrow Road to the Deep North* is a violent piece of work
in which many minority cultures work for the majority culture Japan as the
latter is ruling and has taken the people of minority cultures as Prisoners
of War and makes them work on a railway line for the Japanese people.
At the beginning of the novel, when the Japanese people are in power,
everything works in their favor. But towards the end of the story, the
scenario changes and the people who used to rule one day are presented
for trial and are jailed. The now ruling government sentences these people

for life imprisonment to be hanged till death. Choi Sang-min is a Korean character who is brought up in a Japanese-ruled country. In his childhood, he was forced to be alienated as he, being a Korean, is not accepted by the Japanese and is punished by the Japanese for speaking in his native language that is Korean. As he grows up, he decides to leave both cultures voluntarily when he realizes that if he says that he belongs to the dominant country, he will get fifty yen,

> "*I am not Korean, he thought to himself. I am not Japanese. I am a man of a colony. Where is my fifty yen? He wanted to know. Where? (347)*"

He realizes that he has no particular identity as he has been named differently by people of different cultures. This loss of identity is a result of the uncertainty of belongingness with any one culture. Initially, it is forced by the Japanese people who are dominant and ruling, and then the withdrawal is voluntary. The doll is the protagonist of the novel *The Unknown Terrorist*. She belongs to a minority culture and is ashamed to be a part of that culture. She works as a prostitute and always pretends to be a part of the dominant white elite culture by always running after brands. She even changed her name given by her culture of origin that is Ginna. "I grew up like a cat, my friend... My friend has no hand in it. You know any cats with an interest in family history?" (7)

Later in the novel and a few years later in her life, she realizes that the culture she has been admiring throughout her life is not worth liking as she comes to know that no one in the dominant culture is worthy of all the love and affection she usually shows to them and their culture. She chooses to die in the end because of the aftereffects of being alone and rejecting both cultures. *The Sound of One Hand Clapping* is again a novel that gives us some instances where we can see some characters alienating themselves, withdrawing their association with any of the cultures prevalent around them. Bojan, the father of the protagonist Sonja, loses command over his mother tongue and could never learn the language of the dominant society or the culture. He says to Sonja, for whom he considers the English language that is the language of the dominant culture to be very important, "Perhaps you say this because you have plenty of words... You find a language. But I lose mine. And I never had enough words to tell people what I think, what I feel. Never enough words for a good job." (39)

He lies in an abyss as he belongs to nowhere. He clears his thinking about their belonging to one particular culture when he replies to Sonja's wish to return home. He says, "Where? What home? You and I have no home. Don't you understand? ... We have a wog flat, my Sonja. A wog flat. Don't you understand?..." (374) In the same way, the chaos going on in the mind of Sonja, the protagonist, can be seen when she finds it challenging to figure out how she should address her father. Finally, she settles down halfway and addresses her father as "Dad" (37). This word is foreign to Bojan and Sonja, which belongs neither to Slovenia, the culture of origin, nor Australia, the dominant culture.

Apart from marginality, Berry gave another type of marginalization that is deculturation, according to which, the decision to remain aloof from the dominant as well as the culture of origin is forced upon the people of a minority culture or the weak culture by forcing them not to participate in any of the events of either culture. This discrimination starts from the institutions like the institute of education. First, the people of the dominant culture do not let the children of the mi8nority culture live peacefully in the educational institutes. Then this discrimination takes hold of the elders of the dominant society troubling the peaceful lives of the people of the minority culture. The significant difference between marginality and deculturation is that there is no hope left in the latter, leading to more psychological issues in the weaker culture. Thus, there is "withdrawal" and "apathy" (20) without any pressure. There are instances of this type of marginalization in a few novels by Richard Flanagan.

In the novel *Death of a River Guide*, the protagonist Aljaz tells us that there was a time when local black aborigines of Australia and the white convicts became free settlers because they were not allowed to migrate to the land of the dominant culture that is white. The people made a new race and gave birth to the children of the other culture but belonged to no one culture. This condition resulted from the dominant white culture's unique and strict rules and regulations forbidding blacks from entering their domain. They made sure that the blacks were also away from their culture of origin by forcing the white convicts to stay with the blacks. The result is that the natives of Australia or the weaker section now lie between two cultures without their will. Similarly, the forced decision by the people of the dominant on the people of non-dominant culture can be seen in the novel *The Narrow Road to the Deep North*. The story is all about the violence by the ruling culture that is the Japanese culture on the nondominating or other minority cultures who are taken as prisoners of war by the Japanese and are assigned the task to build a railway line for the Japanese so that the latter may spread their rule over other countries also. The novel is also about the pathetic condition of the camp and the people of minority cultures living and struggling with diseases in those camps. Later in the story, the ruling culture becomes the non-dominant culture, and those who earlier used to work under their rule are now the dominant ones. A Korean character named Choi Sang- min holds some position in the Japanese government when the latter is ruling. But later, when there is a change in the conditions, the readers are told that it is the second time that this character feels as if he is nothing and belongs to no particular place. Earlier, the dominant Japanese people ensured that whosoever talked in their mother tongue other than the Japanese was punished severely. Choi Sang-min is punished as he is caught by the Japanese authorities whispering in Korean. This behavior makes him feel as if he belongs to no particular culture. He is neither entirely accepted by the Japanese people nor is even carried away from his cultural origin. Later, when the Japanese are no more in rule, he senses "in the Australians the same contempt for him that he had known in the Japanese" (322). The conditions make him confess that he has no identity and that he belongs to no particular culture (348).

In the novel *Gould's Book of Fish,* Mr. Lempriere is a white character posted as an official in the black aborigine community with some unidentified task. The conversations that he does with other characters show that he is not accepted by the Royal white society that he craves to be accepted by. He lives amidst the black Australian aborigines but initially keeps himself *segregated* and proudly maintains his culture of origin, and openly rejects the culture of the majority. Although he belongs to the white society, he is rejected by the culture of majority and minority. As a result, he is found to be struggling to be accepted in the culture of the majority. Even after killing many black aborigines to prove his worth to the royal society, he is still rejected. He hence is alienated by the will of the dominant culture. Similarly, William Gould, the novel's protagonist, "lives like a rat" (42) wherever he goes because the dominant culture always rejects him.

In *Wanting,* Robinson, who is white and is given a task by the white society to civilize the black Australian aborigines and make them behave like whites so that the culture of whites becomes more widely accepted, is one of those characters. But he is accepted by neither the whites nor the blacks. He is marginalized throughout the novel. He is forced to live under such circumstances that he cannot associate himself and his family with any culture (61). Similarly, Mathinna is the black aborigine protagonist, who, in the beginning, seems to be very lucky as she is adopted by the white governor Mr. John and Lady Jane and gets a chance to live with the whites in their society and is given a chance to learn the culture of the dominant people. But she finds her culture of origin to hinder associating herself entirely to the dominant culture. When the white people realize that she cannot be tamed and trained according to them, they throw her in an orphanage where she loses her identity as she is neither a white nor a black now. She remains like this throughout her life. Lady Jane once says, "Rather than getting better quickly, as one might have expected with a white child, she has grown worse." (173) Mathinna is now like a pet according to the whites, neither black nor white (173).

The Sound of One Hand Clapping is also a novel that gives us a few instances of deculturation. There is a minor character named Jiri, who travels a lot in the world. "In Czechoslovakia he had drink with the gypsies. In Tasmania he drank with the aborigines. He was never accepted by either, but then he, being half Sudeten German, half Czech, had never felt accepted anywhere." (114) Jiri feels rejected everywhere as wherever he goes, the dominant culture leaves him, and till that time, he loses his own culture also. He thinks that "like the Roma and the blackfellows he had never had any other choice." (115) Like Jiri, Bojan, the father of the protagonist Sonja, feels rejected and alienated as he thinks that the dominant culture has never accepted him and that the people of the dominant culture also makes him leave his culture of origin leave behind by putting a condition that if he wants to grow, he needs to get rid of the past and the past culture. His daughter Sonja observes that "her father now wore clothes that spoke of nowhere, nothing, nobody, cheap clothes that were neat but shiny with wear, suggesting nothing more than a desire for comfort and warmth, of protection against the cold." (20)

The characters in the novels mentioned above face difficulty, a life full of negativity. Some reject the dominant culture, and some are forced to be away from the dominant culture and maintain their culture of origin. In contrast, some of them leave both cultures behind with their own will. Some are forced to take this decision by the dominant culture by keeping the people of the minority cultures to participate in any event of the dominant society.

The present thesis studies the cultural identity and identification. The characters from all seven novels have been studied in detail, and the struggle to maintain their identities is explicitly elaborated in this chapter. The aim of the present chapter is to explore intricacies of acculturation in the fiction of Richard Flanagan.' The effects of the previous two processes given by Berry, segregation and marginalization, have been studied in detail with the two types of each of them offered by Berry. According to Berry, segregation has two sub-divisions- self- segregation or rejection and exclusive segregation. In the former type, the characters maintain their culture of origin and reject the adoption of the majority's culture. In the latter, the dominant culture people force the characters to take this decision. One of the few characters who fall in the category of rejection is Sonja, the mother of the protagonist of *Death of a River Guide*, who marries an Australian man but rejects to adopt her husband's culture and maintains her original culture.

Similarly, Colonel Kota, Rooster MacNeice, Jack Rainbow, and Nakamura, a few characters from *The Narrow Road to the Deep North*, which work for the dominant culture, hate them, and proudly maintain their root culture and reject to be a part of the dominant culture. Language plays a significant role in the novel *The Sound of One Hand Clapping* for showing the love for origin and hatred for the dominant culture in the minds and hearts of the characters of a minority culture that migrate to Australia for a better future. Twopenny Sal is the best example of self- segregation or rejection' as she kills her children that she gives birth to in a foreign land, and the children of her foreign owners who force her to be a part of them leave her culture. But her violent decisions prove the level of love and attachment for her culture of origin and hatred for the dominant culture.

There are various examples of the second type of segregation as well. For example, the treatment of the non-Australians by the native Australians in *The Sound of One Hand Clapping* and the treatment of the non-Japanese by the ruling Japanese pressurize the people of minority culture to segregate themselves. Similarly, Boy, grandfather of the protagonist of *Death of a River Guide*, faces severe discrimination by the native school children and even the school teachers. This behavior of the majority of people around the little school-going boy forces him to be away from the people of the dominant culture and be limited to his culture of origin only.

Marginalization similarly is divided into two types- marginality, in which the characters are seen to keeping themselves aloof from both the original and the dominant culture without any pressure, and deculturation, in which the characters were observed to be forcefully separated from their culture of origin and also not accepted by the dominant society. The characters like Walter Talba Bruney and Robinson in *Wanting*, Doll in *The Unknown Terrorist*, and Bojan in *The Sound of One Hand Clapping* fall in the category of the former type, while the characters like Jiri in *The Sound of One Hand Clapping*, Choi Sang-min in *The Narrow Road to the Deep North*, Mr. Lempiere in *Gould's Book of Fish* and Mathinna in *Wanting* fall under the category of the latter type of *marginalization*.

The aim of the fifth chapter is to apply the theory of Acculturation and Orthogonal Cultural Identification. The remaining processes of the theory of acculturation as given by Berry are practically applied in this chapter. The processes of segregation and marginalization have different implications of effects on two different levels that are individual and societal. One thing that is common in both of them is that the results are negative on both levels. At the individual level, self-segregation has different effects on the psychology and inner health of the individual. Self-segregation or rejection leads to an isolated self in which the person makes his life difficult to live peacefully due to his orthodox and unchangeable mindset. He soon gets frustrated with his life and the people around him as he becomes unacceptable by the people of the dominant society. He finds it difficult to adjust after a while.

On the other hand, if the process of segregation is forced upon the dominant society, the individual gets depressed very quickly. He fights from his inner self due to the pressure and the treatment he gets from the people around him. This struggle leads to more frustration, and as a result, the individual might opt for suicide as the only way out to run away from the humiliation and the inner chaos. Marginalization, like segregation, is negative, but the former have comparatively more negative results. At the individual level, on the one hand, marginality, in which the individual moves away from both cultures with their own will, leads to a life full of struggles within. On the other hand, there is no one around with whom the individual can share the way s/he feels, which further leads to many psychological issues. Initially, the individual might feel thrilled by the decision, but he might find himself lost in the world all alone later in life.

Similarly, deculturation, in which the decision to leave behind ones' culture of origin and reject the culture of majority or dominance is forced upon by the dominant society, leads to complete loss of identity. The treatment by the people of the dominant culture makes it intolerable to live in such a painful and struggling atmosphere. If weak from within, the individual might choose to suicide, and if strong from within, he might raise his voice against the injustice, and the treatment s/he gets.

The above-discussed processes have different effects on the second level that is societal. Society as a whole gets affected by the subdivisions of the two processes. For instance, self-segregation or rejection of the dominant culture by the individual or group of people and the decision to maintain the culture of origin without any pressure leads to slow or zero growth rate of the society. There are no modifications in society. Even if the dominant culture people want the minority culture to mix up, the society remains monotonous. The growth rate remains the same in the second subdivision of segregation that is 'exclusive segregation.' Still, the latter can also lead to more chances of social unrest because of the revolt of minority groups to get equal rights and better treatment. Marginalization is the most negative of all as there is no hope left in the people of the minority culture to grow or sometimes even live. Marginality leads to a non-growing society as the people decide to live alone. There are very few chances of social unrest in this case, whereas, in deculturation, there are many chances of internal riots and social unrest. There is no scope for the development of the society as the people of the dominant culture do not want the people of non-dominant culture to mix up and grow with them.

Marginalization is of two types- Deculturation and Voluntary. Segregation also has two types- Self segregation and Exclusive segregation. Social harmony and progress depends on how the groups are treated and howthe process of identity formation is processed. The dominant culture reflects itself in language, food habits, culture as well asin state policies.

CHAPTER FOUR

Orthogonal Cultural Identification

Culture is a very complex term that cannot be defined in one way that is acceptable to all the scientists and scholars. Nevertheless, this idea is what Oetting, Donnermeyer, Trimble, and Beauvais had to convey in their 1998 research. They have enlisted some qualities of culture that seem to be a part of many definitions of culture that various eminent scholars have given in their studies.

1) Culture is a body of knowledge, attitudes, and skills for dealing with the physical and social environment passed on from one generation to the next. 2) Cultures have continuity and stability because each generation attempts to pass the culture on intact. 3) Cultures also change over time as the physical, social, political, and spiritual environments change. (2081)

The mode of retention of the culture has been termed as enculturation, and the mode of cultural change has been termed acculturation. The definition of both these terms will be discussed later.

The first significant confusion related to the term identification is the difference between the terms identity and identification. Grammatically, both the terms are nouns but there is an abstract difference between the two. The term identity means a state of self that one presents to the world, or in other words, what the world knows an individual to be, is the identity of that individual. In contrast, identification is the process of being identified as a particular individual. For instance, the scar on the leg of Odysseus proves to be a sign of his identity. It helps identify him being Odysseus by the lady who washes the feet of this stranger and even the father of Odysseus to recognize him as his son who has been a wanderer for 20 long years. Now, what does cultural identity mean? Repeating the definition of Hill from 2012, igi-global.com stated that, "Cultural understanding and appreciation for the cultural diversity that exists across nations and the multiplicity of worldviews that results from it is essential to developing international-mindedness." On the other hand, cultural identity is the process of being identified as a member of a particular culture.

There has been much debate as most people use the terms 'Cultural identity' and 'ethnic identity' interchangeably. However, the fact is that both these terms differ in meaning. On one hand, cultural identity is when people of a group or an individual have a sense of belonging to a particular culture. In contrast, ethnic identity is a sense of belonging that relates a group of people from another group or an individual to another. Thus, cultural identity is an umbrella term that includes a social and ethnic identity. Jane Collier and Milt Thomas combined the ethnography of communication and social construction to frame the properties of cultural identity. These properties refer to how the members of a group communicate their identity. According to onlinelibrary.willey.com, Identity Negotiation Theory defines identity as "an individual's multifaceted identities of cultural, ethnic, religious, social class, gender, sexual orientation, professional, family/relational role, and personal image(s) based on self-reflection and other-categorization social construction processes." The concept of identity is vast as it includes many aspects of an individual's life. Some of the elements that help an individual to get an identity by which he is identified as an individual by the members of his society are religious beliefs, personality, attitude, social status, age, sex, gender, race, caste, political affiliations, profession, sexual orientations, etc.

Orthogonal cultural identification theory was given by Oetting and Beauvais in 1990-1991 research paper. These authors have been particular while defining the term cultural identification. In order to understand what cultural identification is, it is vital to know what it is not. These authors want us to understand that cultural identification should not be mixed with ethnic and cultural identities. Ethnic identity, according to Oetting and others in the year 1998, is a social construct that has been long associated with race. (Oetting et al 2086) According to these authors, generally, ethnic identity is based on the geographical location one belongs to, but it has many subcategories. One may feel offended when someone specifies his/her ethnic identity. It has been found familiar with the Japanese and the Koreans.

When the authors talk about the closest association of cultural identification, they choose cultural identity over ethnic identity. In his 1993 paper, Oetting gave a crisp definition of cultural identity, which was used as the base for the model of orthogonal cultural identification given by Oetting ad Beauvais in 1991. Oetting, in 1991, stated that cultural identity is the process of identifying an individual who belongs to a particular group that can be "of a national culture, of the culture of religion, of the drug culture, or even... of a specific marriage." In the 1991 paper by Oetting and Beauvais, the authors present a new viewpoint altogether. They compare the papers and the theories given by the scholars before them and conclude that no matter how advanced a theory is, "people are still placed somewhere between cultures" (661). According to Oetting and Beauvais, an individual can adopt the traditions, rituals, values, and beliefs without losing the traditions, rituals, values, and beliefs they already hold of any other culture. The bicultural models given till now allow the immigrant or the person from a minority culture to maintain both cultures simultaneously. However, these models do not acknowledge that there can be any difference between the degrees with which the individual feels the connection with both cultures.

Orthogonal Cultural Identification is a theory that is centered on a pluralistic society. In the words of a writer whose article is published on psychology.iresearchnet.com, Orthogonal Cultural Identification Theory argues that individuals may identify with more than one culture without necessarily sacrificing one cultural identity for another in a pluralistic environment. The central element of this theory is that identification with any one culture is independent of identification with other cultures. Therefore, cultural identification can be distinguished from ethnic self-labels or ethnic group categorizations, such as Latino/a, Mexican, American Indian, African American, and European American.

The theory has more relation with a pluralistic society rather than a multicultural society. The difference between the two similar seeming terms is that the latter lacks the presence of a dominant culture. It means that a multicultural society, like a pluralistic one, has more than two cultures living together, but unlike the latter, the former has no dominant culture. The model of orthogonal cultural identification is straightforward to understand. The figure given below is the modified version of the original diagram given by Oetting and Beauvais. The changes that have been made are minor, like the word 'Alienation' has been omitted and the labels of some in the diagram have been replaced from a culture-specific term like 'Native-American' and 'Hispanic' to more general terms like 'Host-culture' and 'Culture A' respectively.

ORTHOGONAL IDENTIFICATION

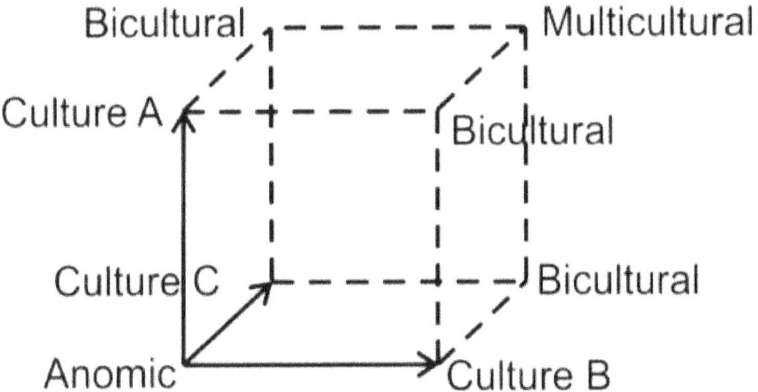

Figure 4 : Oetting, Eugene R., and Fred Beauvais. "Orthogonal cultural identification theory: The cultural identification of minority adolescents." *International journal of the addictions* 25.sup5 (1991): 655-685Figure 4 : Oetting, Eugene R., and Fred Beauvais. "Orthogonal cultural identification theory: The cultural identification of minority adolescents." *International journal of the addictions* 25.sup5 (1991): 655-685

The figure demonstrates the idea of the authors that an individual may have belongingness with different cultures without actually affecting the degree of belongingness to any other culture as they orthogonal that is non-related. Oetting and Beauvais, in 1991, pointed out:

"*Any pattern, any combination of cultural identification, can exist and... any movement or change is possible. There can be highly bicultural people, unicultural identification, high identification with one culture and medium identification with another, or even low identification with either culture, (662)*"

'Anomic' refers to a person with very little to no identification with A, B, or C cultures. Moreover, an individual who maintains his belongingness to any two of the three cultures is shown by the dotted lines and are mentioned to be 'Bicultural.' Those who have some relation to all the three cultures that are more than two are also depicted by the dotted lines and are mentioned to be 'Multicultural' at the top right corner of the cube. Every corner of the cube shows its orthogonal nature, which means that no two aspects are related to each other in any way.

There has always been a sense of doubt at and controversy in the previous theories related to any identity an individual adopts living in a particular bicultural or multicultural environment. However, the theory given by Oetting and Beauvais explains every little doubt that has ever existed in the readers' minds. Moreover, the previous theories put an individual in water-tight compartments, that is, either he could go this way or that way. The person who belonged to the minority culture was the one, according to these theories, who had to change or adjust. However, in that matter, the theory by Oetting and Beauvais is way too flexible and open as it talks about all the loopholes of the previous ones. Apart from the theoretical part of this model, Oetting, and Beauvais, in 1991, gave Orthogonal Cultural Identification Scale, most commonly known as OCIS. The main aim of designing this scale was to measure the degree of the belongingness of an individual with more than one culture. For this reason, the questions asked in the scale have four options which ultimately lead to a quantitative measurement of the qualitative degree or the depth of belongingness or the cultural identity.

Timothy A. Lower published a paper in 2008 wherein he applied the OCIS on the Asian Indian international exchange students to study the variety of meanings given to the items in the scale. In this paper, he mentions that OCIS "has been used in Mexican American (Oetting & Beauvais, 1990-1991b; Oetting, Swaim, & Chiarella, 1998), Native American (Oetting & Beauvais, 1990-1991b; Oetting et al., 1998), Asian American (Johnson, Wall, Guanipa, Terry-Guyer, & Velasquez 2002)9, and African American (Strunin & Demissie, 2001) populations" (33-34). The figure below is a modified version of the scale initially given by Oetting and Beauvais in 1991, and a sample of only one question is presented.

1. Some families have special activities or traditions that take place every year at particular times (such as holiday parties, special meals, religious activities, trips or visits). How many of these special activities or traditions did your family have when you were growing up that were based on ...	A Lot	Some	A Few	None At All
White-American or Anglo Culture				
Mexican-American or Spanish Culture				
American-Indian Culture				
Black-American Culture				
Other culture. Please specify:				

Figure 5: Oetting, Eugene R., Randall C. Swaim, and Maria Carla Chiarella. "Factor structure and invariance of the orthogonal cultural identification scale among American Indian and Mexican American youth." *Hispanic Journal of Behavioral Sciences* 20.2 (1998): 131-154.

There are eight questions in total and six out of them give a flexible opportunity to the individual being tested to express their opinion from the four given options. The last two questions have only three options: 'yes,' 'no,' and 'don't know'. The scale has been used multiple times, and the results are pretty satisfactory.

According to a paper published in 2012 in the 'Global Centre for Pluralism,' various countries have successfully incorporated pluralism in their societies. Canada is considered to be the best example of pluralism. However, some have consistently failed at their attempts at maintaining a pluralistic society like Kenya. There are around 40 ethnic groups in Kenya who divide themselves into majority and minority groups. No particular group has full majority powers with them. The major reason that is known to be behind the failure or the success in maintaining a pluralistic society is 'state control' and 'the policies,' which are framed in the best interest of all the cultures living together and are appropriately implemented. Richard Flanagan's novels have various characters who believe in the maintenance of a pluralistic society.

Cultural identity can be identified by various elements like dressing style, language, accent, and beliefs. *The First Person* by Richard Flanagan shows almost all of the above said signs to judge the cultural orientations of an individual. In this case, the first instance could be of one of the most remarkable criminals of Australia named Siegfried Heidl. Heidl is born somewhere in remote Australia. His parents are not very well to do. He chooses to be a criminal for money. He goes to Germany and does very petty jobs to earn money. However, he adopts the German accent, and this accent stays with him till his last breath. He travels America also, and this country gives him the dressing style that stays with him until he lives. When Kif, the protagonist, meets him for the first time, the former is disguised. As Kif is an aspiring author, he is hired by a company to write Australia's one of the most remarkable criminals Siegfried Heidl. The disguise of Heidl gives an impression as if he does not belong here. "... the beard, along with the American basketball jacket— an oddity in Australia—seemed to be about drawing attention rather than evading it." (85) Heidl and Kif have a telephonic conversation before they meet. On the phone, Kif imagines Heidl to be a person with "a soft voice" and is from Germany because of his "accent a light German." (85). Apart from the dressing style, Heidl adopts the popular terminology with the majority culture in America.

Kif, the protagonist, and Heidl are alone in a room where Kif attempts to get complete information about the latter's life. Kif expresses his feelings and says that he is happy to stay back late and work with him. Heidl reacts to Kif's expression very late, but when he replies, he says, "Roger that, Kif" (85) which is an American military saying for 'I agree.' There is one more instance when Kif and his best friend Ray, who works as an assistant to the criminal Heidl, sit and drink together, and just by one action of Ray, Kif is reminded of the way Heidl speaks. Kif thinks "of the odd way Heidl said mate, with his strange half-American, part-German voice with its Strine overlay" (221). Heidl comes out to be a character whose orientation to one culture does not affect the degree of his orientation to any other culture. He mixes his culture of origin that is Australian, the majority culture in America and Germany.

Kif is the protagonist of *The First Person* and is born in some remote area of Australia where it appears from his behavior later as if the culture and traditions practiced by them are pretty different from the rituals and belief system of the majority culture of Australia. He seems to be an aspiring author who is in desperate need of a job as he has responsibilities of his wife and his three children. Once, he gets a call from a famous company in Melbourne, which is located in the mainland southern part of Australia. He gets a job to write a biography of one of Australia's wanted and dangerous criminals, Siegfried Heidl. He is scared to say yes, but he relocates from remote Australia to mainland Australia as he has bills to pay. He finds it quite different there. The way people dress, the lifestyle, the accent, and even the belief system of the majority culture people. However, slowly with time, he adopts the values and beliefs of the people of the majority culture. However, this does not affect the degree of his belongingness to his root culture or the culture of origin.

The Unknown Terrorist is another beautiful novel by Richard Flanagan, which has a story of a dark girl Ginna, who is known as the Doll throughout the novel. She has a low-income family background and this is why earning money becomes her only goal in life. She moves to Sydney, Australia, and starts working as a prostitute with the same purpose in life. She does not consider this profession wrong, but she finds it difficult to sleep with different persons every night. She is very fond of brands. She dreams of buying a branded handbag and tells her friend that she has saved money for this Louis Vuitton handbag. One day, when she and her best friend Wilder go to a beach for the latter's son to have a perfect space to play, the former meets a tall, dark and handsome man named Tariq. Tariq saves the life of Wilder's son and from that moment on Doll feels attracted to that man. Soon the two develop a romantic relationship. They make out in his apartment, but in the morning, Doll finds a note that said "Had to fly. Call you soon." (85) After some days, the Doll finds out that Tariq is a terrorist and that the cops of the town are in a search for him. Just because of that one night, the Doll gets in trouble as she is seen with Tariq in the CCTV cameras.

There is a minor character named Frank Moretti, a pretty but disabled art collector. He pays the Doll for private sessions to do pole dance, but he gets very intimate and cozy with Doll and takes out the benefits of the money he pays to the Doll. Frank Moretti is Italian by birth. However, good job opportunities bring him to one of the elite areas of Australia. Nevertheless, his culture of origin does not affect the equal effect of the French culture on his accent. He uses both accents quite well when he speaks English. "It was as if he believed he belonged to some higher race of beings who understood Beauty and Art, who took holidays in Tuscany, and made an odd noise like the rolling of snot in the back of their throat when pronouncing Italian or French words." (128) Apart from the cultures mentioned, as he is now in Australia, he wants to adopt the lifestyle of the Sydney people who are in the majority. Later in the novel, he develops a soft corner for the Doll or Ginna Davies. When the cops come and ask him about the girl, he lies to the cops. While greeting the cops, he does this in the exact what of how Sydney people do. "It was in any case, his way with authority, his Sydney way: to smile, help, offer hospitality and friendship." (194). Frank Moretti is a person who has a culmination of three cultures in him. However, all three cultures are orthogonal to each other. The degree of his belongingness to one out of three has no relation with the degree of his belongingness to any other of the remaining two cultures. Although he is a minor character of the novel, apart from him, the other characters show no signs of adopting more than two cultures without getting the affiliation to other cultures affected.

The Narrow Road to the Deep North is a booker prize-winning novel with many layers of stories running parallel. The protagonist of the novel is Dorrigo Evans, who is an Australian aborigine. He is a well-educated man who serves as a doctor in the Japanese POW camp. The story takes an exciting turn when Dorrigo indulges in a two-sided love affair with his uncle's young wife. He gets many chances to make this relation more and more intimate. Richard Flanagan's life's many incidents are depicted in this novel, and hence the novel is semi-autobiographical. Apart from his love life with his aunt, he has a loving wife who never doubts her husband. However, Dorrigo does not feel the same way with his aunt Amy as he finds himself addicted to the curves and fragrance of the latter's body. This part is one side of the novel.

The second side of the novel is ruthless. The Japanese government attacks the weaker countries, takes the people defeated as prisoners of war, and makes them work as slaves day and night, starving for food and living in very unhygienic conditions. There are people from different countries who live together under one roof and have good relations. However, some people carry hatred and prejudice in their hearts for the people they live with and belong to the countries they hate. As a result, people die of hunger and diseases that are very painful and awful to look at. Dorrigo tries his best to save as many people as he can but sometimes finds himself helpless. The role of the supremacy of the dominant culture is very vital in giving shape to the novel. The Japanese are dominant and decisive in most of the novel. They treat other people as sheer waste and as non-humans. For instance, they can beat up an individual in the middle of so many people gathered around. However, the people, who want to come forward and help, find themselves helpless as the beaters belong to the dominant and influential culture.

Similarly, in the latter half of the novel, when Japan gets out of power and America comes into the scene, the same Japanese who used to practice their power are now forced to be quiet and mum and behave according to the rules and regulations now powerful America. However, some characters like Major Nakamura are and have always been proud of being from Japan. Even after the downfall of the Japanese government, when he shifts to America to live a more peaceful life, he says when asked that he is Japanese and is proud to be, with the fact known that being Japanese is not quite acceptable because of the tortures that Japanese did in their golden period. However, some characters change their identity wherever they go and whatever is the demand of the situation.

Dorrigo is an Australian but he is pretty open and flexible about the culture he follows and the other cultures he comes in contact with. Although, as mentioned earlier, he is quite educated and intelligent, he seems to have read a wide range of literature and history. He mentions at many places that he is fond of Greek legends for whatever they have done in the past. One day, he and his lover, his aunt Amy, decide to take a room in a hotel and make out. He also mentions that "Greeks are our heroes. They win." (10) In this conversation, Amy and Dorrigo are discussing the Trojans and the Greeks. When Amy asks why considering Greeks to be their heroes, Dorrigo has no specific answer to it. This incident shows the psychology of Dorrigo, who considers intercultural relations and connections to be perfectly all right. He has read about the culture, values, traditions, and belief systems of the Greeks. He has also adopted some of them without affecting the degree of belongingness to his own Australian culture. Apart from the Greek culture, Dorrigo seems to be influenced by the American culture also. Nevertheless, the degree of his belonging to the American culture has no relation to his belonging to the Greek and Australian culture. "He drank— why would he not drink? A few whines at lunch, sometimes a whisky in his morning tea, a negroni or two before dinner (a habit he had picked from an American significant while with the occupying forces in Kobe) and wine with it..." (385)

The prisoners of war are from different countries and hence follow different cultures. Even after the harsh attitude of the Japanese with them and the torture given to them for being from a minority culture, they still seem to love the culture of origin. When they are taken to the Japanese land to build a railway line for the Japanese so that the people in power find it easier to spread their empire, they show some signs of having some degree of affiliation with other cultures than theirs. That degree has no relation to the degree of belonging to their culture of origin. The Australians, including Dorrigo, are going to the Japanese POW camp when they find that Americans have attacked them. However, just before they are attacked, they plan to have "French coffee." (35) This example shows the adoption of the lifestyle and habits of people of other cultures. Apart from this incident, there are various others in which the minor characters of the novel are found practicing the culture they do not belong to and also loving their culture at the same time without the love for native culture getting affected. Rooster MacNeice is one of those minor characters who have this sort of psychology towards the diversity of cultures and the beauty of these cultures in this diversity. He practices his culture of origin as he has always been practicing in the POW camp. However, apart from his own culture, he seems to be interested in German culture. He seems to love Adolf Hitler and the rules and regulations and the lifestyle of the people there framed due to the strictness of the ruler. He reads the book 'Mein Kampf' regularly and tries to learn one page daily.

Before he was even properly awake, Rooster began that morning as he did every morning, with the first of several exercises in the self-discipline which he knew would ensure his survival, mentally, physically, and morally. He commenced by reciting under his breath the page of *Mein Kampf* he had memorized the last night before. (191) During a conversation with a minor character Tom, Dorrigo comes to know that Old Jackie's wife is a black aborigine. This idea comes as a shock to Dorrigo as the latter knew only one thing about that lady: her Spanish blood. However, the wife of Old Jackie has maintained both cultures so that the people around her do not know the other culture that she practices. This example means that the degrees of belongingness to each culture were orthogonal and had no relation to each other.

> *"Old Jackie, said Tom. Goodfella. Best of blokes. Knew the bush. His wife was a blackfella, you know? For a moment or two, Dorrigo couldn't place Jackie Maguire's wife at all. Then a long-dormant memory... Though he had heard vague tales of aristocratic Spanish*

blood, one of the traditional Tasmanian alibis, Dorrigo hadn't know she was an aborigine... (406)"

It has been noted for ages that the ones who are in power and who belong to the dominant culture try to pressure the people from the weaker cultures or the cultures of the minority to either accept the traditions and rituals of their culture or bear the discrimination that is done by the people of the dominant culture through various institutions of the society like marriage, education, jobs, etc. The same thing happens with the prisoners of war. By expressing his superiority in being from the dominant and ruling culture, a Japanese officer tries to influence the minority people and asks them to feel proud to be serving this culture (41). In such circumstances, some may feel like adopting the dominant class's tradition, values, and rituals. However, some start feeling more repellent after being pressured and hence are ready to accept the torture and even death but not bow down from the dominant culture. Darky Gardiner is one of the notable characters in the life of the protagonist Dorrigo. Under the strict rules and regulations of the Japanese government, Darky makes his bed the way they are taught by the Japanese in the latter's style (198). Although this is an example of forced assimilation, the increasing degree of belongingness to the Japanese culture does not affect the Australian culture of origin. Hence, Darky, here, is an example of Orthogonal Cultural Identification.

Similarly, according to Major Nakamura, people of inferior culture, like Chinese, Europeans, and Indians, are addicted to opium. This opium is a part of Japanese culture. However, the fact that these people have adopted the majority's culture does not change the degree to which they belong to their own cultures of origin. Later in the novel, when the war is over, the Japanese officers who once used to be a part of the dominant and the ruling culture are now hiding. Major Nakamura and Colonel Kota are two such examples hidden in America because they have come to know that they are on the list of war criminals and are being hunted. Despite the fact that they are in America, they still preserve the culture they originally belong to. They live the American lifestyle and have entirely adopted the latter's culture to look like them. However, again, the degrees of belongingness to each of the two cultures have nothing to do with each other. It means that they are orthogonal or are non- relatable.

There is one more minor character named Colonel Rexroth. He is from Australia that becomes a minority culture when he is captured by the

Japanese as a Prisoner of War. Whenever he addresses the prisoners of war, he uses "pukka accent" (43), an elite accent used by the British. Two things need attention here. First, the degree to which he belongs to the Australian culture has no relation to the degree of identification with the British culture. Second, there is no relation between the dominant Japanese culture and the other two cultures. This instance shows the orthogonal nature of Colonel Rexroth's identification with multiple cultures.

Then there is one more masterpiece by Richard Flanagan and that is *The Sound of One Hand Clapping*. This novel revolves around Sonja, a three-year-old protagonist at the beginning of the novel, whose parents have shifted from Slovenia to Australia in search of better food, a better job, in short, a better lifestyle. Since the beginning of the novel, the readers are informed that Sonja's mother and her father are uncomfortable with the new environment but are forced to adjust to dominant Australian society. The politician of the area indirectly pressurizes the immigrants or the people of minority culture to forget their shameful and poor life and adopt the ways of Australia. If they want to be happy and earn money, they need to do as per the sayings of the politician. It is not only the politician who forces or pressurizes them; instead, he is also the voice of all the people of the dominant culture. The poor immigrants have no choice but to agree with the people of the dominant culture. Maria leaves the town leaving behind her three-year-old daughter Sonja and her husband, Bojan. She does not return to her home ever. Bojan starts drinking and soon decides to leave his daughter to his friend's family and earn money. Nevertheless, he loves his daughter very much. Sonja faces many issues in the new house she had to shift to. In the beginning, everything goes well, but soon the lady of the house starts feeling as if Sonja is a burden if the latter does not help in the household chores. The former's husband now starts feeling for the twelve-year-old Sonja. He tries so many times to touch Sonja and make intimate relations with her forcefully, but he fails repeatedly. He even goes to the extent of calling her mother a prostitute because, after Maria leaves, people start assuming that she ran away with another man and betrayed Bojan.

This novel runs back and forth in time. Even the names of the chapters are named after the years of the incidents described in the chapter. The novel starts in 1954 when Sonja is three years old and turns sixteen in 1967. Then the story jumps to the year 1989 when Sonja turns thirty-eight years old. Now when Sonja is a grown- up older woman, we know that she has left her father back in Tasmania and shifts to the elite area of Australia, Sydney.

She visits her father, and on her way back home, she is surrounded by all the memories still alive somewhere in her brain. Mostly, she remembers the bad memories associated with Tasmania. Bojan has now become an alcoholic, which he was before also, but now, as Sonja finds out, he has forgotten everything. He has no purpose in life to look forward to. He drinks day and night. The character of Bojan has not been that of a good father from the beginning of the novel; instead, he beats his wife and also starts beating his daughter after his wife leaves him alone.

Sonja has suffered in her childhood like her mother. The Sonja family hails from Slovenia that is captured and brutally ruled by the Nazis. The condition of the poor people of Slovenia is very pitiful. The Nazis make them dig a hole that needed to be accurate in the size they say, and if not, they make the person squat in the hole and fill the hole back just leaving the head of the victim out of the ground and then kick the head like a football till the victim dies a painful death. Maria Buloh, Sonja's mother, is raped at the age of twelve and is then made to watch the murder of her mother with her own eyes. Sonja, likewise, is sexually assaulted by her uncle, with whom her father Bojan leaves her to stay till the time he goes in the town to earn enough money for both of them to stay together. The experiences of her mother and those experienced by her shape the cultural identity that they form. Not only this, Sonja gets betrayed by two men in Sydney when she is away from her father. The second shock comes along with many difficulties as she gets pregnant with the second man. After knowing that she has conceived, she travels back to Tasmania to tell her father about her condition with a hope that now, after so many years, her father would accept her child with open arms. Nevertheless, she faces strong rejection by her father. The past here invades her life again, and the cycle starts again. However, slowly, with time, she convinces her father and gives birth to a baby girl that brings much happiness to a family that has never been happy after Maria Buloh left the house.

The family of an individual plays a significant role in shaping her/his the mind and the future. Bojan and Maria try from the beginning to give the best to their only daughter. Language has played a vital role in this novel to identify various characters with many cultures. As mentioned earlier, Maria leaves the house when Sonja is just three years old, but she makes sure that her infant daughter learns the language of their roots, Slovenia. She recites some lullabies in the Slovenian language that Sonja remembers throughout her life. After knowing that if an individual does not know good English s/he cannot succeed, her father brings many books, including Encyclopedia Britannica, so that his daughter becomes fluent in the language of the majority culture. However, he also ensures no effect on the degree of identification with the culture of origin as the degree of identification with the majority culture increases.

Like other novels of Richard Flanagan, culture is the least explored aspect. Nevertheless, a few characters in the novel show the signs of the orthogonal nature of identifying with the various cultures they have adopted like Bojan. He belongs to Slovenia and loves the Slovenian traditions, values, rituals, and belief systems. He loves it so much so that he maintains the degree of this identification throughout his life. However, he also maintains the belongingness to other cultures.

> "*Before drinking, Bojan gives the obligatory Slovenian toast—'Nostrarvia!'—and they both took a few sips. 'Is it good, eh'? Bojan said. 'Apricot schnapps and leatherwood honey. Us and them. He laughed at this unlikely union of central European drink and Tasmanian food. (57)*"

Not only the degrees of these three cultures, but he also maintains a balance with that of Turkey. For example, Bojan enjoys having "Turkish coffee" (183). Bojan is one of those characters who are open to change but are loyal to the previously held notions. Bojan meets so many people throughout the novel and learns their culture also. His American neighbors give him their culture's food habits, so he asks Sonja to prepare the American food their way only. However, this open-to-learning nature of Bojan does not affect the degree of his belongingness to the Tasmanian or the Slovenian culture. Apart from these cultures, he knows Italian culture also. language comes out to be an essential aspect of a culture that promotes it and spreads the love for culture. Bojan includes Italian phrases in his Slovenian, Tasmanian and American vocabulary. For example, in a state of complete drunkenness, Bojan speaks the Italian phrase "Madonna Santa" (389), which means good gods. However, other languages are not affected due to the accent of the Italian language.

> "*... he was back in the FJ and the motor was misfiring and rattling as he was driving into the heart of the town., and he was just hoping to Christ that it got him there and praised it in Slovenian (Dobra staryr*

auto) for all its years of faithful service and beseeched it in Italian (Per favore cara macchina) to last the few more miles that would see their journey finally ended and ordered it on Deutsch (Raus! Raus!) to continue going and cursed it in Australian (shitfuckingbucket) for spluttering worse than himself in the morning. (412)"

This balanced mixture of the languages of various cultures shows the orthogonal that is non-related nature of the belongingness to more than one culture. Not only Bojan but there is one minor character also which shows the exact nature of cultural identification. Jiri is a character who spends most of his life among Gypsies and hence adopts their lifestyle and habits. "Like the Gypsies, he used several masks: of speech, of behavior, of personality." (115) Pavel is another character which is attracted to various cultures and adopts some or the other thing from all of them. He keeps on talking about the various cultures he has in and what he knows about them. However, the fact is that the degree of belongingness to one culture has no relation the degree of belongingness to any of the other cultures. Hence, they are independent of each other, and there is no effect of the traits of one culture adopted by him on the traits of the multiple other cultures he belongs to.

Moira Heaney is the daughter of an American family which comes to live next to the Bojan family. She is almost Sonja's age and hence they befriend each other. Sonja, who is a Slovenian, teaches Moira some Slovenian words and in turn, Moira teaches her the American accent that Sonja carries and uses throughout her life. These two girls mix one or the other aspect of the other cultures than theirs and do not let the degree of belongingness or identification get affected at all. This case shows the orthogonal nature of identification. When he smells the American food next door, Bojan asks his daughter to prepare it for him and mixes the Slovenian way with it, and enjoys his meal. Even on her sixteenth birthday, Sonja prepares food in a style that suits the tastes of people of both the cultures: Australian and the Slovenian.

Orthogonal Cultural Identification does not necessarily mean that an individual can have affiliation with or identification to multiple cultures. He may also choose to keep none. This case is acceptable only if it is his/her choice not to affiliate or identify with any cultures. In this case, identifying with one culture will not relate to the degree of identification with another culture. This case may not be applicable when the dominant culture rejects an individual or a group and the feeling of alienation arise; it is the case of deculturation.

Gould's Book of Fish is a masterpiece in itself. The book is written in twelve chapters which are printed in different colors, where each color signifies something. This novel is based on the real-life experiences of a convict in Australia. William Buelow Gould is the protagonist of the novel and also an unreliable narrator who alternates the narration with Sid Hammet. This novel has very little to do with the storyline and the characters. Instead, Gould's protagonist travels the places, and most of the novel is about his thought process. Sid Hammet is the one who finds Gould's version of the book of fish. He reads it, and when he plans to research it and tell people about the actual history of the penal colony, he forgets it on the counter of a pub. He has no proof of what he read. He stares at a fish. Now, this fish has become very important. The second part of the story revolves around the actual experiences of Gould. It is tough to trace the background of Gould for two reasons; one, he does not know who he is, and second, he denies what he has said before and hence is a very unreliable person. However, all he knows is that he is a son of a man whose name is unknown to everyone and who slept with Gould's mother, who died during childbirth. He starts working at a place where there is a heavy load of work, and hence he runs away to London and finally lands in Tasmania after traveling the whole world. Tasmania was a penal colony back then.

In America, Gould meets a man named Jean-Babeuf Audubon, who is an artist. Earlier, before meeting the latter, Gould never wanted to be a painter, but somehow he learns it and starts using the identity of a painter whenever he falls in a troublesome situation and has now come to know that being an artist can save him from any difficulty. For example, a desperate prison doctor named Tobias Lempriere hires him to paint some popular fish of the Macquarie Harbor. However, unfortunately, this doctor is so desperate to get a seat in the Royal Society that he starts killing black aborigines, cutting their heads off the body, and preserving the skulls of these black aborigines considering that the white people in the Royal Society will like this work of research. However, Gould just used an artist's identity faking to be a painter, but now he realizes that he is an artist and starts painting from his heart and soul.

Gould is hired by many people who are not happy with his work and this way, finally, he lands up in prison where he is hired by a prison doctor. The prison in which Gould is kept is flooded twice by the seawater as it is in the basement and near the sea. Gould gets a chance to swim in the flooded prison and reach the record cell of the prison. He realizes that the history is written for the world to read about the penal colony does not tell the actual brutal nature of the officers and the sufferings of the prisoners who are arrested without any crime. Instead, history glorifies the rulers' success and how effectively they rule the colony and control the criminals. Gould ensues in a fight with the record cell officer in the record cell and swims out from the place in a complex condition. However, he finally succeeds in escaping the prison and hides in the interiors of Tasmania, where something magical happens, and Gould realizes that he has now become a fish. Now, Gould, in the form of a fish, is the same fish that Sid Hammet is staring at.

Gould falls in love with a black aborigine on the island whose name is Twopenny Sal. Although she has a minimal role to play and nothing to contribute in the story of fish by Gould, she turns out to be an essential character from the perspective of the superiority and inferiority of cultures and the power and brutality of the dominant culture, and the helplessness and the sufferings of the people who belong to the minority culture. Twopenny Sal catches the eyes of some white men who decide to take her to their country as a full-time slave. When they come to know that she will never agree to go with them, they kidnap her son and condition that they return her son only because she accompanies them. She finds herself very helpless and agrees to their condition, having no choice to say no. The moment she lands in the area dominated by the whites and from where she could never return to her land on her own, the white masters kill her son by smashing his head on a rock. Twopenny Sal is now alone, helpless, and betrayed in a foreign land, where no one will ever listen to her. She gets pregnant with her masters many times but takes her revenge by killing her children which she gave birth to by the white masters. She becomes a perfect example of a black aborigine woman who, when decided, can do anything even in a foreign land where she has no one whom she can call hers.

William Buelow Gould travels the whole world like Odysseus and learns and adopts several aspects of different cultures he comes across. He mentions himself, as he is the narrator of the novel also, apart from being the protagonist,

> "*I learnt also—though more from the birds Jean Babeuf Audubon failed to shoot than from Jean-Babeuf Audubon himself... Thus in*

*America, I learnt the value of being an underworld Englishman,
while later back in the underworld England, I played upon being and
American adventurer, and here in Van Diemen's Land nothing more
than an Artist From Elsewhere—by which, of course, I mean Europe,
no matter how mediocre. (412)* "

Gould states that he behaved according to the situation. That very clearly means that the degree of his identification with the American culture has no relation with the degree of his belongingness with the British culture. This is the orthogonal or the non-related nature of his cultural identification. Apart from the two cultures mentioned above, Gould seems to have incorporated the French culture into his identity. He says, "... that feigned interest was returned with more French Martinique rum... initially thought was very good... inclining to believe excellent" (124). The degrees of identification with the three cultures have no relation with each other. Apart from the three cultures, American, English, and French, Gould has also incorporated the ancient Roman and Greek language and lifestyle. The belongingness to all of them is orthogonal. There is one more culture that Gould associates him with or, in other words, with which he identifies himself, that us Dutch. He says, "...on that canvas we danced the old Dutch still life, rolling waxen pears and bursting pomegranates and me a dead limp hare at the end of it all" (114). He develops a taste for the art of Dutch masters and hence incorporates their style of painting in his. The degrees of identification with which he identifies are non-relatable to each other.

A minor character named Mr. Hung is a Buddhist by religion and worships various French legends. He, who considers Victor Hugo to be a God, also worships the French legends (8). The degree of association with the belief system of one culture does not affect the degree of that of the other one. The general black women of Australia, who are proud to be an aborigine, have adopted the belief system of the white culture. They believe that those black aborigines who die are reborn as Englishmen (340). This attraction shows the superiority of the dominant class. However, it also shows that those women, who have a certain degree of identification with their own culture, the culture of origin, also have a certain degree to which they have identified with the culture of the dominant class or the dominant culture. Twopenny Sal is a character who is taken to a foreign land by force, but she learns the language, incorporates English words, and then uses English and Aboriginal words. The degree of her identification with the dominant culture is not affected by her identification with her culture of origin (271). Tracker Marks is another character whose degree of association with the American culture does not affect the degree of his association with the Australian culture as he is a black aboriginal Australian. He dresses like the American whalers, but his belief system and the tradition he follows are still the same as his culture of origin (219).

Richard Flanagan's *Death of a River Guide* is a novel which has a description of three generations, narrated by the protagonist Aljaz Cosini, who is drowning in the river and has been granted visions in which he can see the life of his father, his grandfather and many other people that died before his birth. Aljaz comes to know about the history of Tasmania in his visions as he sees the history of the members of his family. The plot of the novel is a complex one as he narrates the stories at three different levels. One, his birth in Italy till his drowning in the river during a river expedition, second, the story of the experience of the river expedition and third, the story of his father Harry and his mother Sonja and also of his grandfather Boy when Harry is a kid, due to which, the author had to use the kaleidoscopic technique that is narration running back and forth in time. Aljaz works as a river guide that pays him significantly less, and he decides that this expedition will be the last one, after which he will settle and do something else. However, fate has some other planning for him. He drowns and dies slowly, witnessing the history of Tasmania and the members of his family.

Aljaz is made to believe that they immigrated to Australia with their own will, but through the visions, it becomes clear that they have a convict ancestry and have not descended from a white man. A convict named Ned Quade used to be who escaped the prison and looked out for shelter here in Tasmania. This incident fills Aljaz with a sense of more belongingness to the land than he ever felt before. With the history of his ancestry, Aljaz also envisions the history of Tasmania till the present day. It shocks Aljaz that the fact that has been told by the histories is wrong. The books of history tell us that all the black aborigines were either shifters or murdered and that there are no black aborigines in Tasmania anymore. However, the fact is that they still exist.

The love life of Aljaz is not peaceful at all. He is in love with a girl named Couta Ho, with whom he also has a daughter. Their lives are envisioned by the drowning Aljaz. They are thrilled as Couta gives birth to a baby girl, but their lives change completely after their infant daughter dies. Couta holds

Aljaz to be responsible for it and cannot overcome the grief of the loss. There comes a gap between the two. On the one hand, Aljaz wants her to come out of the grief and tries his best to keep her away from Jemma's memories. While on the other hand, Couta finds it challenging to get off that pain. She starts lying to her husband. She says that she will attend knitting classes to move on and her husband allows her to. However, in the name of knitting classes, she continues visiting her daughter's grave. Moreover, when she realizes that she is about to get caught by her husband, she buys two sweaters from the market, one for Aljaz and one for her dead daughter. She shows Aljaz's sweater to him and tells him that she has knitted it with her own hands. She starts believing that her husband does not understand her and can never really feel the pain and grief she is going through because she is the one who bore the girl inside her for nine months. She had all the attachment to her as she was the one who stayed with Jemma day and night and not Aljaz, who was always out for work.

The river trip that proves to be the last trip for Aljaz begins when Aljaz is forced by his boss to go on the expedition being an experienced guide. He meets a fascinating character here named Cockroach, who is a co-guide with him. The first few days are spent with fun and there in peace with all. However, after some days, they find themselves stuck on small forest land. When they plan to leave, Aljaz warns them that the river will be flooded as it will rain heavily. All of them consider his point and plan to stay longer, till the weather clears up. However, the next day, they depart their journey, and the weather betrays them. The river is flooded, and they are stuck in the flooded river. On their way, a traveler, who is in their boat and their responsibility too, falls in the river and flows with it. Luckily, he takes hold of a tree stem that keeps him falling from the fountain. Aljaz takes this responsibility and decides to save him. The traveler becomes a firm believer in Christianity and hence leaves his hands believing that Christ will come and save him. However, his body is lost as the co-travelers, and the guide tries to find his body everywhere. Finally, there comes the point where Aljaz drowns in the water and keeps on going down. No one can see him or his body, but he can hear the voices of the policemen and the people on the shore. Aljaz realizes that his life and the life of other members of his family start moving in from his eyes. And then he realizes that he is not dying despite being drowned for so long because he has been granted visions. Through the visions, Aljaz sees the life he has already lived and the lives of his father and grandfather, and even the first ancestor of his family. He also envisions the actual history of Tasmania that is hidden by the history creators.

Aljaz is born in Italy, but his parents shift to Australia when he is a kid. It is shown that the Cosini family is told by everyone that their ancestors are white and they have nothing to do with the black aborigines. However, while drowning in the river, Aljaz sees the truth of his ancestry, which is from a criminal named Ned Quade and not from any white. However, Aljaz and his family enjoy the class of not being an aborigine throughout their lives. On the river expedition, Derek asks Aljaz what they are planning to eat that night, to which Aljaz replies, "Ekala... a traditional Brazilian dish" (132). Apart from this, Aljaz enjoys sipping "Turkish coffee" (246), which he makes on his own. The degree to which Aljaz is associated with the multiple cultures is not related to the degree of association with them individually. This is the orthogonal nature that is the non-related nature of the belongingness of Aljaz with more than two cultures at a time. The degree of association with the Italian culture of origin does not change even slightly by the increase in the degree of association with the other two cultures.

Lou is sent to interview the crim who lives in Fitzroy, a suburb in Australia. Crim's culture of origin is unknown, but the cultures he associates himself with are shown through his eating habits and lifestyle. "... only went out twice a day, once to shop at the Vietnamese store up the road, the other to eat tea at a Syrian Cafe" (29). The mixture of these two cultures is so up to the mark that it seems that he belongs to both the cultures equally as the degree of association with any of the cultures has no relation to or is not affected by the degree of association with the other culture(s). Maria Magdalena Svevo is the second mother to Aljaz as she helped his mother during his birth. Although she is an Italian and the degree of her belongingness with it is pretty high, her affiliation with the Australian culture does not affect the former degree. She enjoys having Australian cigars only and has incorporated them into her lifestyle (5). Aljaz was brought up in Australia and knows Australia's culture very well, and he belongs to the Australian culture. However, he uses Italian phrases repeatedly throughout the novel that shows that he is also associated with the Italian culture to a certain degree. He says, "Madonna Santa" (226) again and again, which means 'my goodness' in Italian. However, the degree of his association with the Italian culture does not affect the degree of his belongingness to the Australian culture. Similarly, a minor character in the novel named Reg, the husband of Aunt Ellie, is a black aborigine. He plans to complete the construction of his house in Australia with the material and the style that is popular in America (193). There is a certain degree of identification with the American culture, which has orthogonal nature and hence has no impact on the degree of association with the Australian culture.

The last novel by Richard Flanagan till 2019 is *Wanting*. This piece is a beautiful novel that tells the story of the effects of two or more cultures mixing up. There is a little black aborigine girl named Mathinna, whose other name is Leda. She is christened with the name of Leda by the protector, who is assigned the task of civilizing the black aborigines by the ruling and the dominant people of white culture. For this purpose, the protector makes a colony of some houses built up in the way of the whites and teaches the black aborigines the lifestyle of the whites. The black aborigines are given food eaten by the whites so that they get habitual to it. Towterer is the father of Mathinna but lives away from her as she is taken by the protector, and Towterer could not keep him from taking his daughter away.

Towterer is a strong character who believes in the culture of origin despite all the pressure made by the whites to adopt the white culture and leave living like 'animals.' But when his wife dies, Towterer saves the eyes of the whites and cremates her as is done in his culture rather than burying her, which the dominant culture teaches (67). Robinson, the actual name of the protector, goes to the living place of Towterer and other black aborigines, who are yet freely moving, to capture them according to the strict orders of the white government. The night he reaches there, Towterer and his party remove his clothes, blacken his face, and dance around the fire as they do. When Robinson wakes up, he sees that Towterer and the party have left the place with his gun along with them. Later in the novel, he tries to convince Towterer by blackmailing him emotionally in his daughter's name and saying that she needs you and so you should come along. However, Towterer declines his idea and leaves again with his party, but before leaving, he says that he trusts Robinson that he will take care of his daughter.

Mathinna is a black but charming girl who catches the eyes of Mr. John, the governor of the white government, and Lady Jane, who is so mesmerized with the beauty, dance, and red dress of Mathinna that she decides to take Mathinna along and civilize her on her own. Mathinna gets ready as she always wanted to be like the whites and learn the magic that only whites knew; that is the art of writing. She tries a lot, but she could not leave the traits of her culture behind and be entirely like the whites. Lady Jane throws all her weapons that she was using in civilizing and taming Mathinna. She says to her maidservant, "For the black child would not become white." (174), But she adopts a certain degree of the white culture and has a certain degree of belongingness to the culture of origin till the end of the novel. However, this particular degree of association with the white culture goes to the extent that Mathinna counts the number of fathers. "There was God her Father, and Jesus his Son, who was also a sort of a father there was the protector, who had the Spirit of God the Father; and then there was Sir John, who was also her father, her new father—so many fathers." (120)

Mathinna, at a party, is supposed to wear an English dress and behave like the people of the dominant culture behaved. Although she wears an Italian dress as she was expected to wear, she sings and dances in her culture of origin style only (13). The degree of identification with the white culture does not affect the degree of her association with her culture of origin. Her company is quite toxic and gives a new face to her teacher, Mr. Francis Lazaretto, from Sydney. She teaches him aboriginal songs and the way of dancing (128). But the degree of association with aborigine culture does not affect the degree of his association with his Australian culture of origin because of the orthogonal nature of the cultural identity.

Cultural identity and identification have been studied in this chapter. Orthogonal cultural identification has been traced in the works of Richard Flanagan, and the theory of orthogonal cultural identification has also been applied. The various cultural identities of the various characters and the variety within the cultures are studied. In the first novel, *First Person*, there is a significant character named Heidl, the most wanted criminal of Australia. He adopts various cultural identities, but it is observed that no particular identity affects the forming of another cultural identity. He is basically from remote areas of Australia and has a certain degree of association with that culture. However, he also associates himself with other cultures like American and German. He associates himself with the German culture to such a degree that he adopts a German accent to his language. He belongs to American culture also to a certain degree in which he adopts the dresses he wears. However, the degree of identification with American or German cultures does not impact the degree of belongingness to his native culture. Similarly, it was found in other novels that the relationship of the strength of relation to one culture is not at all related to the strength of relation to any other.

In the novel *The Unknown Terrorist*, Frank Moretti is one of the notable characters of the novel who play an essential role in giving a turn to the life of the main protagonist, Ginna or the Doll. Moretti is Italian by birth, this is his cultural identity, and he believes in the traditions and the rituals of Italian culture very strongly; this is his cultural identification. However, when he moves to Australia, he adopts one more cultural identity and adopts talking and greeting people. He is also associated with the French culture, as he uses a French accent in his language. However, the degree of association with one culture has no relation to the degree of belongingness to any other culture. In the novel *The Narrow Road to the Deep North*, Dorrigo, the protagonist, is an Australian but is captured and works as a surgeon to the prisoners of war from various countries in the Japanese POW camp. He has a certain degree of association with the Australian culture, which neither affects the degree of his identification with the French culture. He likes having French coffee and American culture as he has adopted many American habits in his lifestyle.

Bojan Buloh, the protagonist's father and one of the main characters of the novel *The Sound of One Hand Clapping*, includes Italian phrases in his Slovenian, Tasmanian and American vocabulary. For example, Bojan speaks the Italian phrase "Madonna Santa" (389), incomplete drunkenness, which means good gods. However, there is no effect of the accent of the Italian language on the other languages that he uses.

> "*... he was back in the FJ and the motor was misfiring and rattling as he was driving into the heart of the town., and he was just hoping to Christ that it got him there and praised it in Slovenian (Dobra staryr auto) for all its years of faithful service and beseeched it in Italian (Per favore cara macchina) to last the few more miles that would see their journey finally ended and ordered it on Deutsch (Raus! Raus!) to continue going and cursed it in Australian (shitfuckingbucket) for spluttering worse than himself in the morning. (412)*"

All these cultural identities possessed by Bojan are not related to each other and do not affect the degree of belongingness to any one of them. In *Gould's Book of Fish*, William Buelow Gould has adopted various cultural identities, as he belongs to American, English, and Australian culture with the degrees varying in each culture. Apart from it, he belongs to the Dutch culture to a certain degree that is not related or orthogonal to the degree of belongingness to the other cultures. Aljaz, the protagonist of *Death of a River Guide*, belongs to Italian, Australian, French, and Turkish cultures. The degree of strength he belongs to varies and does not affect the degree of belongingness to any other culture.

The effect of Orthogonal Cultural Identification is different on an individual and at societal level. At the level of an individual, unlike acculturation, as it is very flexible, the individual experiences a perfect condition of mental state. S/he experiences inner peace and can achieve her/his personal goals with much more effectiveness. S/he is free to have any degree of cultural identity and enjoy any number of cultural identities as s/he pleases. This condition gives liberty to the individual to mix up in the society and form strong relations with people around her/him. It allows them to interact more and adopt the good things of different cultures. On the societal level, orthogonal cultural identification also helps form an ideal society where every individual is at peace and has no discrimination. The dominant culture is very flexible, and so is the minority culture. As the people of the dominant culture are also free to adopt or have more than one cultural identity, it leads the way to a peaceful society. Apart from the peace in the society, it becomes an ideal society that grows continuously as the people are not investing their energies in showing the other one inferior and themselves superior; they focus more on the growth of the society as a whole.

The process promotes growth of the individual as well as of the society as a whole as this process is less about competition and more about association. Mental state of the people involved also remains intact because of the liberty to practice many cultures at a time. The immigrants face challenges and changes in their cultural orientation whichleads to a new identity formation.

CHAPTER FIVE

Psycho-Social Intricacies

Acculturation is defined as a process that occurs when two cultures come in contact. Many models have been given in order to understand the process of acculturation. Berry's four-fold model is said to be the best in bi-dimensional phase models, as all the other models have one or the other loophole that caught the eyes of the critics. John Widdup Berry gave this model in his 1974 research paper. According to this model, the immigrants, who form the culture of minority, have four options, better known as the strategies or processes of acculturation, to opt from while coming in contact with another culture- assimilation, integration, segregation and marginalization. According to Robert E. Park and Ernest W. Burgess, social behavior has four categories, out of which assimilation is one and the three others being conflict, accommodation, and competition. It is "a process of interpenetration and fusion in which persons and groups acquire the memories, sentiments, and attitudes of other persons or groups and by sharing their experience and history are incorporated with them in a common cultural life." (735)

Berry has given two sub-categories of assimilation, namely melting pot and pressure cooker. On the one hand, melting pot is a process in which people of a minority culture or the immigrants leave the culture of origin and adopt the tradition, values and rituals of the dominant culture with their own will and without any external or internal pressure. Talking about melting pot, he says that it is a voluntary action on the part of the immigrants where "...whenever an immigrant group accepts the goals of the new society and is willing to adopt the patterns of the new society to attain the goals." (19)

On the other hand, pressure cooker is the process in which the people of the dominant culture pressurize the people of minority culture to adopt their culture while cutting off from the latter's culture of origin completely.

Similarly, the process of integration also has two sub-categories- democratic pluralism and paternal integration. According to the process of integration, the people of the minority culture maintain both the culture of origin and the traits of the dominant culture with or without any pressure. The first sub-category that is democratic pluralism is the process in which there is no pressure on the people of the minority culture to maintain both cultures. In contrast, in the second sub-category that is paternal integration, it is the wish of the dominant culture that the minority culture maintains both the cultures. The third alternative for the people of minority groups or immigrants is segregation, which, when applied to a larger society, was termed separation by Berry. According to him, segregation can be practiced in one of two ways- one is when there is no pressure to say no to the adoption of the majority culture, which he termed as self-segregation or rejection. In Berry's own words, rejection or self-segregation is the decision pattern in which "...the ethnic group(s) affirm their culture and identity but deny the usefulness of positive intergroup relations. Among highly acculturated ethnic groups, this pattern is often referred to as "reaffirmation"..." (19)

The other one is when the people of majority culture do not want the people of minority culture to mix with them or behave like them and so create an external pressure either by banning them from entering their social institutes or by discriminating and misbehaving with them in public which he termed as complete segregation. The fourth and the last alternative with the people of the minority culture is marginalization, which is the most negative of all. The people of minority cultures do not align to any particular culture that is neither the culture of the majority nor the culture of the minority. Marginalization, according to Berry, is of two types- marginality, where the immigrants reject their belongingness to both the cultures by their own will and the other, deculturation, where the people of the dominant culture do not let the people of the minority culture identify with any one culture that is neither with the dominant one nor with the non-dominant one.

The Orthogonal Cultural Identification Theory is a pluralistic theory that bases its principles on the fact that in a society, variety of cultures co-exist and that an individual adopts one or the other trait from two or more than two cultures. It is very flexible as it considers that every individual is free to adopt any trait with any degree of strength without letting the degree of his/her identification with other cultures or cultures.

The proponents of the theory, Fred Beauvais and E.R Oetting, gave a scale to measure the degree of one's identification with different cultures and whether the increase in the degree of affiliation to one culture affects the degree of his belongingness to any other culture or cultures. This scale has eight questions where the last two have three options to answer from, whereas the rest are answered from four given options ranging from 'A lot' to 'None at all'. The answers are then analyzed, and the results are arrived upon. The scale has been successfully applied to various surveys. The result is that the increase or decrease in the degree of identification with one culture does not affect the degree of belongingness to any other culture/s. Thus, there can be any reason for a society to be successfully pluralistic or fail. According to a paper published in 2012 in the 'Global Centre for Pluralism,' various countries have successfully incorporated pluralism in their societies. Canada is considered to be the best example of pluralism. However, some have always failed at their attempts at maintaining a pluralistic society like Kenya. There are around 40 ethnic groups in Kenya who divide themselves into the majority and minority groups. No particular group has full majority powers with them. The major reason that is known to be behind the failure or the success in maintaining a pluralistic society is 'state control' and 'the policies,' which are framed in the best interest of all the cultures living together and are correctly implemented. Oetting and Beauvais in 1991 point out,

"Any pattern, any combination of cultural identification, can exist and... any movement or change is possible. There can be highly bicultural people, unicultural identification, high identification with one culture and medium identification with another, or even low identification with either culture, (662)"

Intricacy, according to www.dictionary.cambridge.org, is "a detail that is part of something complicated." According to Merriam Webster dictionary, intricacy is "something that makes a situation more complicated or difficult." Some synonyms of the term intricacy are 'complexity,' 'complicacy,' and 'complication.'

Berry's model of acculturation, which has four strategies or the processes, has both social and psychological effects. Both the cultures involved in the process of acculturation get changed in one way or the other. Some changes are negative and some positive. However, most of the changes that have been observed in various studies occur in the minority group or the people of the non-dominant culture. The researchers also found that the dominant society's political power and the political condition play a significant role in shaping the cultural identity and the after-effects of the acculturation process. Berry published a paper in the year 2001 in which he pointed out

> *"If it is assumed that high contact always and inevitably leads to low cultural maintenance, then the only possible outcome of intercultural contacts is the absorption of one group into the other with the melding of the two into a blended culture, leading to the disappearance of distinct cultural group. (617)"*

Berry here talks about the social effects of acculturation when the people of minority groups are cut off from the culture of origin and merge with the dominant culture, and he calls this process assimilation. This way, each process has a different effect on two levels, one being social and the other being the psychological level of the individual identifying with the culture of the minority. At the social level, the complexity created by the melting pot is, as Berry also mentioned, that the society loses its pluralistic trait, which means that when the people of minority group leave the culture of origin and merge with the dominant culture or adopt the traits of the latter, the diversity of cultures in the society is seen no more. This pattern will slowly lead to the slow growth of society as a whole. The positive change that will happen in the society after this process is that there will be complete peace in the society as there would be only one culture left. Berry published another research paper in 2011 in which he gave a diagram depicting the condition of the society in melting pot that clearly defines the social effect of this process.

MELTING POT

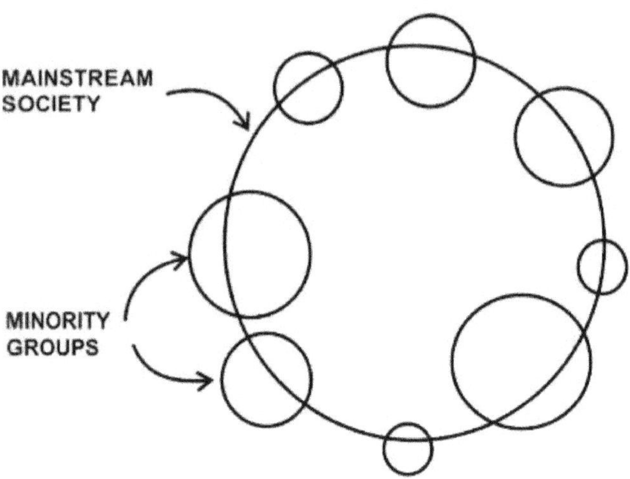

Another process of assimilation, according to Berry, is pressure cooker which has different implications on the societal level. As the definition of pressure cooker states that there is an external pressure that is exerted on the people of minority culture to get away from their culture of origin and adopt the tradition and values of the dominant culture, there are total chances of internal conflicts that may lead to social disturbances like riots, protests, etc. In this situation, society will have hardly any chance to develop. Political power also plays some role here. The influential people in the political system of the dominant culture and those who want their culture to spread everywhere might pressure the non-dominant culture to forget their previous lives and start a new life by learning the lifestyle of the people of the dominant culture. Assimilation also has positive effects on society, like the social peace that will persist after the process. It will help the dominant culture gain popularity with the increase in the number of its followers. There will be the formation of a new *cultural identity* for the people of the minority group.

Berry's concept of integration has two sub-categories based on the question that is whether the choice of maintaining relations with the dominant culture and also keeping the roots of the culture origin is made by the people of the minority culture or is this choice is forced on them by the people and the institutions of the dominant culture. In the case where the choice is made by the immigrants by their will and which is termed by Berry as democratic pluralism, the effect on the societal level is positive. A new language will take birth that will blend the languages used by the people of both the dominant and the non-dominant cultures. Apart from forming a new language, the society will have a speedy growth as a whole as all the members of the society will have no cultural differences. Whereas, parental integration or inclusive segregation, in which the people of the non-dominant culture are pressurized by the dominant culture to maintain good relations with both the cultures, there is a possibility of a threat to the internal security of such society. Not only does it affect society as a whole, but it also affects the psychology of an individual from the minority culture a lot. The latter case in integration may lead to many behavioral changes like aggression, a sense of losing one's own cultural identity that s/he has been holding till the dominant culture forced them to integrate, etc. It may further act as a cause of the state of depression in the people of minority cultures. He stated in his 2001 paper,

> "*...there is a rather easy transition involving both "culture shedding" and "culture learning": Individuals change the way they dress, what they eat, their greeting procedures, even their values by reducing (suppressing, forgetting) one way of daily living and taking on replacements... Outcomes can range from conflictual and stressful contacts and relationships to those in which mutual accommodations are achieved. (620)*"

However, in the former case, of democratic pluralism, the psyche of an individual from the minority culture will be at peace as it is her/his choice to integrate. The people of the minority culture are usually seen to have experienced *double consciousness*. The individual will experience the presence of two identities with them and sometimes find it quite confusing where they belong, leading to *identity confusion*. According to Berry, there is one more possibility here. He states in his 2001 paper that if the people of the dominant society do not want the integration process to occur, there would be no *mutual integration*. Hence, the people of the dominant culture might trigger the feeling of *alienation* amongst the people of the non-dominant group. The sense of alienation can further trigger the feeling of homesickness amongst the people of the minority culture. However, there are more favorable than adverse effects of this process of integration. The *cultural competence* of the individuals of both the dominant and the non-dominant cultures increases with time. An individual basically can interact, work effectively and make meaningful relationships in a pluralistic society. Such a society will be able to practice a pluralistic approach successfully.

According to Berry's four-fold model of acculturation, the third process is segregation, which is based on whether it is a choice or a pressure to reject the majority culture and maintain one's own culture, divided into two sub-categories- self-segregation or rejection and complete segregation. The latter sub-category of segregation negatively impacts the individual's psyche, identifying with the minority or the non-dominant culture. The individual may undergo acculturative stress, which can cause stress, anxiety, and emotional disturbance as they feel pressured not to mix up with the people of the higher or the dominant culture. In the 1960s, Oberg gave the concept of 'cultural shock,' which Berry, in 1970, considered an inappropriate term compared to another term that Berry introduced, i.e., 'acculturative stress.' He had three reasons for choosing the latter over the former. The first reason is that the latter is closely related to psychology; the second reason is that the term 'shock' brings all the negative impacts on the individual, whereas the term 'stress' might bring both positive and negative. Third, last, and the most acceptable reason is that it is the outcome of two cultures coming in contact that is acculturation and not related to the problems within one culture. Acculturative stress is a response by individuals to life events (rooted in intercultural contact) when they exceed the capacity of individuals to deal with them.

The people of the dominant culture discriminate against the people of a minority culture by not letting them enter the social institutions made for the people of the dominant culture and this social discrimination can cause a sense of alienation and homesickness. It has been observed that many immigrants even commit suicide under such circumstances as there is a constant feeling or a sense of being deprived and cut off from the mainstream. Apart from affecting the psyche of an individual, exclusive segregation also affects the larger society as a whole. Due to the emotional disturbance and the other adverse effects on the psyche of the individuals, some people belonging to the minority culture, being discriminated against and not being allowed to participate in the rituals and the social functions of the people of the dominant culture, sometimes start revolting due to *groups* in the society. This formation of small but revolting groups will then cause chaos or riots in society. Instead of being a multicultural society, it will turn into a pluralistic society but not a successful one. Moreover, society as a whole will never grow or develop under such circumstances. The positive aspect of exclusive segregation is that the people of the dominant class that form the majority of the population in that society feel that their traditions, rituals, and values are safe and will be practiced and transferred with the same devotion and purity as has always been practiced and transferred from one generation to another.

Self-segregation or rejection, on the societal level, does not affect in very negative terms. As the choice of not being associated or identified with the dominant culture is made by the people of the minority culture themselves, there are very few chances of revolt and riots in such a society. The society would be peaceful in comparison with that of exclusive segregation. However, society will not be able to grow and develop as it could have if it were the case of integration. Political parties, as well as the policies of the government, according to Beery, can further worsen the situation that hinders the overall growth of society. The psyche of the individuals who have rejected to have any identification with the more significant or the dominant culture is very severely affected by this acculturation process. He might experience the signs of inferiority complex, depression, stress, anxiety, and emotional disturbance. There is a sense of hatred and prejudice in the hearts of the orthodox people of minority culture. The sense of alienation, anxiety and prejudice leads to the formation of groups in society, hindering the growth of society as a whole. However, there is also a positive aspect of this process. The individuals who choose to segregate themselves have a strong sense of identification with the culture of origin they maintain and feel proud of.

The fourth process of the process of acculturation, according to J.W. Berry, is marginalization which is again divided into two sub-categories, namely- marginality, where the people of the non-dominant culture decide not to be identified with any of the two cultures, and deculturation, where there is an external pressure by the dominant society stopping the formers from participating in the latter's institutions and various social functions and also not allowing the people of minority culture maintain their culture of origin. At the societal level, both of them have a negative effect. Society will not develop as there will be various smaller cultural groups with hatred for each other. There would be communal riots and chaos within the larger society as the smaller groups will get offended easily. There is a possibility of increasing the death rate due to society's situation and the acculturative stress that the individuals will go through. In the case of marginality, there are fewer chances of internal disturbance due to the lack of pressure felt by the cultures of the minority. However, the people in such circumstances can easily take everything on their culture and attack the people of the larger society with the feeling of prejudice. India is the best example of this, as some groups in the society do not want to be mixed up in the dominant culture or adopt any trait of the latter but are super sensitive to the cause of their culture. Moreover, hence cause internal chaos and social riots, which in India are known as religious riots. However, in the case of *deculturation*, due to the pressure of the dominant culture, the people of the non-dominant culture are filled with the feeling of revolt as they are cut off from even entering the primary social institutions of the dominant culture like education. Therefore, there is no positive impact of the process of marginalization on society as a whole.

At the individual level, marginality has specific psychological effects that lead to severe issues with the individual. For example, there is constant stress on the mind of the individual of the minority culture due to the economic crisis as s/he finds it extremely difficult to get a job and settle in life because of his own decision not to adopt the traits of the dominant culture. It can happen quite possibly because of the orthodox nature of the individual. However, the process of deculturation is considered to be even worse for the psyche of an individual who identifies himself with the non-dominant or the minority culture. In this case, the individual might face the maximum number of challenges in terms of mental peace. There is a possibility that, due to the external pressure of the people of the dominant culture, they feel being deprived of every facility and even untouchables. Stress, anxiety, emotional disturbance, inferiority complex, alienation, and depression are other psychological issues that one might face due to the external force created by the dominant culture. Such individuals become very sensitive to everything. There are chances that they take up some wrong steps to show their reaction like suicide to one extreme and indulging in crimes, riots, and becoming anti-social elements due to hatred, aggression, and prejudice.

It has been observed in various studies that young people and infants or even children do not face any issue in adapting to the new culture or maintaining relations with both cultures. It is the older group of people who have a solid connection to their culture of origin and do not want any change in their lifestyle. Berry, in his 1997 paper, talks about all the changes that can happen due to acculturation as he says

"With respect to group acculturation... Biological changes include new dietary intake and exposure to new diseases, both of which have implications for the health status of the whole group...Social changes range from disrupted communities to new and important friendships. Finally, cultural changes (which are at the core of the notion of acculturation) range from relatively superficial changes in what is eaten or worn to deeper ones involving language shifts, religious conversions, and fundamental alterations to value systems. (17)"

Orthogonal cultural identification is a very positive and flexible approach towards interacting with people of two or more cultures. At the societal level, the impact that it gives to the cultural groups is that the society will grow and develop very rapidly as the individuals and the society as a whole are found to be at peace in terms of *cultural tolerance* and *adaptation*. Conclusion: there would be a successful *cultural exchange*, which will lead to *cultural competence* in people of both groups. At the individual level, at some point in time, there are chances of the feeling of homesickness to be born in the minds of the migrants. According to Berry, there can also be the case where the immigrants' sense of *loss of identity* and *double consciousness* emerges. He, in 1997, wrote about one more possibility that an individual may face.

It is possible that conflicts between demands of parents and peers are maximal at this period, or that the problems of life transitions between childhood and adulthood are compounded by cultural transitions. For example, developmental issues of identity come to the fore at this time (Phinney, 1990) and interact with questions of ethnic identity, thus multiplying the questions about who one really is. (21) He said that the individual might find peace out in the society, but it may not be the case within his/her own family. He believes that every family has some older people who find it difficult to make changes in their lifestyle and with time become orthodox. Due to this, they might interfere in the process that his/her younger would want to undergo. This can cause emotional disturbance within the family and in the individual as well.

However, on the positive side of it, the individual may take up a new identity altogether. The individual will grow as a person as he will learn a lot in such an environment. Berry, in 1997 states the thoughts of Murphy, who considers this process of acculturation to be more positive than negative. He states-

> "*Murphy (1965) has argued that societies supportive of cultural pluralism (that is, with a positive multicultural ideology) provide a more positive settlement context for two reasons: they are less likely to enforce cultural change (assimilation) or exclusion (segregation and marginalisation) on immigrants; and they are more likely to provide social support both from the institutions of the larger society...usually make up pluralistic societies. (17)*"

It is considered that the language, dressing style, eating habits, and the thought process of an individual depict the effect of the contact between two or more cultures. It is said that the psychology of individuals shapes the larger group and that the larger group shapes society. In short, the condition of the society and the psychology of every individual that forms it are directly proportional to each other. The characters of the novels of Richard Flanagan are analyzed in the same light where the complexities or the intricacies created due to the process of acculturation and orthogonal cultural identification are focused upon. This study is done on two different levels- the societal and the individual level, where the role of political factors in giving power to the effects is also considered.

At the individual psychological level, the black aborigines in *First Person* by Richard Flanagan suffer the after-effects colonization. During this time, they feel fascinated by the white people or the people of the dominant culture. Berry's concept of melting pot has a pre-requisite that the people of the minority culture choose to adopt the majority's culture and maintain a distance from the culture of origin. The black aborigines leave the culture of origin behind and have a superiority complex over the other blacks who segregate themselves. Kif, the protagonist and the narrator of the novel, is born in the remote areas of Tasmania but goes to Melbourne, Australia, in search of work opportunities. Knowing nothing about the culture of origin, he makes a place in the dominant culture. He realizes a sense of superiority for the fact of being a part of the dominant culture. He never feels *alienated* or homesick once he mixes up with the people of the dominant culture. Similarly, Ray, the protagonist's best friend, feels that his culture of origin is inferior to the culture he now belongs to and finds peace in the new identity that he gets. Both Ray and Kif, who decide to meet in the dominant culture, lose their original identities, find new, superior, and satisfying identities, which they seem very happy with.

Bojan, the father of the protagonist of *The Sound of One Hand Clapping*, struggles a lot to meltdown in the dominant culture. He comes from Slovenia and has now settled in Tasmania, where he comes with his family in search of a better living style and job opportunities. He has a strong desire to get over the culture of origin completely, but he struggles a lot, which negatively impacts his psychology. He knows it to be a matter of fact that if he and his family want a better lifestyle, they need to forget the past and meltdown in the Australian culture. In 1954, when Sonja, the protagonist, is three years old, Bojan struggles to speak in English but speaks in rolling English. The time flies, but Bojan is still seen as struggling to gel with the people of the dominant culture and the dominant language (213). Bojan feels proud to be an Australian and is very happy to leave the traits of Slovenian culture. He is proud to such an extent that he chooses to speak in the English language even when he is alone, and no one is hearing him (110). He keeps on struggling to get where he wants to reach, but this gives rise to the inferiority complex in this character. He loses confidence to speak in public and interact with people. Towards the end of the novel, Bojan realizes the importance of his culture of origin due to the sense of alienation and the pressure of the memories that make him homesick. However, Sonja, his daughter, and the protagonist mixes with the dominant culture very well and faces no such issue as her father because she gets into the new culture. Initially, she feels as if she has melted down in the new culture leaving the culture of origin behind, but later she realizes that she has equal importance of both the cultures in her life. There is no negative impact seen on the psyche of Sonja.

The characters in the novel *The Narrow Road to the Deep North* have negative and positive effects on their psyche. Choi Sang-min, Korean by birth but was brought up in a Japanese-dominated environment. He treats the prisoners of war as the Japanese treat them (323). Although he adopts the features of the dominant culture of his own will, he experiences the *loss of identity* and *alienation* towards the end of the novel. However, Colonel Rexroth, Australian by birth, is proud to call himself British and talks in the pukka accent used by the British (43). He gets a positive impact of the process of melting pot. The Doll, the protagonist of the novel *The Unknown Terrorist*, is a black aborigine. However, she desperately leaves the culture she originally belongs to and pretends to be belonging to the dominant Australian culture by always running after the expensive brands to match the lifestyle of the people of superior culture. However, she struggles throughout her life as she kills herself at the novel's end for various reasons. However, out of all the other reasons, one reason is that the people of the dominant culture never adopted her as part of their culture, and hence they make her feel deprived and alienated.

Mathinna, the protagonist of Richard Flanagan's *Wanting*, is a small girl and catches the eyes of Lady Jane, the wife of the governor of the dominant white culture. Mathinna wants to be like the people of the dominant culture as she is fascinated by their lifestyle, and especially the art of writing that, according to her, is a sort of magic known only to the people of the dominant culture. Lady Jane takes her to England, where she plans to civilize her. Everything goes well initially as Mathinna is fully charged and desperately willing to meltdown in the dominant culture. She feels fascinated by the white culture, but later on, her culture of origin becomes active as she starts feeling homesick and the importance of her original culture and lifestyle in her life after a certain period. In the beginning, when she is attracted to the people of white culture, she tries her best to imitate them and be like them so much that she starts criticizing the black people who belong to her culture of origin, calling them "uncivilized and uncouth." (217) Red color is an all-time favorite of Mathinna but with the fresh wind of the dominant culture takes her choices from her and expects her to dress like French aristocrats (130). But this fantasy aura of the dominant culture is very short-lived. She finds it very difficult to struggle against her culture of origin and dances her native dance in front of the aristocratic people of the dominant culture. Her mind still wants to be like the whites, but as she is unable to do that and all her white masters leave her amid the storm, she becomes a helpless prostitute in the end. All through her life, she wanted to become something that she is not, which seemed relatively easy initially, but she feels the pressure on her psyche and fails to do so. She loses both her identities by the end of the novel as she does not want to be identified with the black aborigines, and the people of the white culture do not want to accept her. She becomes a depressed and lonely soul who does not know who she is and where she is going.

Death of a River Guide shows positive effects of the process of melting pot as various characters seem to be at peace after the meltdown in the dominant culture, leaving the culture of origin. Harry, the father of the protagonist Aljaz, is an Australian who goes to Italy for better work opportunities. There he falls in love with a Yugoslavian girl and marries her soon. Harry willingly suppresses the culture of origin and learns the taste and lifestyle of the people of the Italian culture. For instance, he develops a taste for Turkish coffee that he learns from his wife (247). He finds himself at peace as this step consequently helps his marriage succeed. However, he feels the importance of his culture of origin and can balance the two cultures after some time. Similarly, Maria Magdalena Svevo, a second mother to Aljaz, is an Italian by origin but moves to Australia with Sonja, Aljaz's mother. She starts loving the lifestyle of the dominant culture and decides to adopt the fantasizing dominant culture. She melts entirely in the Australian culture, and as a part of it, she develops a taste for Australian cigars that becomes her taste for life (2). She learns the new culture very quickly and gets a new *cultural identity*, which further leads to the growth of society. One character pretends to be at peace but struggles to prove that she is a white and not a black aborigine. Auntie Ellie, Harry's aunt, scolds and slaps Harry when the latter asks her how she claims to be white as she looks like a black Australian aborigine (201). This character faces this struggling challenge throughout her life, resulting in the mental breakdown and a sense of inferiority complex with the *identity crisis* that comes along. Her state of mind affects the people around her, like her husband.

In *Gould's Book of Fish*, the black aborigines surrender to the dominant white culture on their own as they feel that their culture of origin is inferior to the dominant culture and start feeling ashamed to be associated or identified with the aborigine culture. After the process of assimilation happens, they start feeling superior even to the white people who were taken as prisoners in their Australian land by the authority of the dominant culture. Therefore, they leave the country for the new country they now belong to. Similarly, the black women assimilate with the dominant culture, which gives them new hope and feeling of getting a superior stature in the society. This decision changes the way they think and the way they feel. Their horizon of thinking and learning the traditions and rituals of the new culture increases after assimilating, which gives them a sense of mental satisfaction.

Society also gets affected by the process of assimilation. When the people of the minority culture choose to melt in the culture of dominance, they tend to leave their culture of origin behind. When they do it without any pressure, society as a whole gets affected positively. Kif, for instance, the protagonist of *First Person*, moves away from his culture of origin and merges in the dominant Australian culture of Melbourne. The office he works in most benefits from this change in culture as Kif now wholly identifies with the new culture without any pressure on him. Society moves towards growth and development.

Similarly, Sonja, the protagonist of *The Sound of One Hand Clapping*, learns the traditions and the rituals of the new culture that is the Australian culture and moves away from the Slovenian culture that happens to be the culture of origin. Thus, she contributes to the positive growth of society and promotes and spreads the dominant culture becoming more popular and adopted. On the contrary, Bojan's father cannot wholly meltdown in the dominant culture and is seen struggling, adversely affecting his psyche. But this condition not only affects the mental state of Bojan but the state of the society around him also. People of the dominant culture, who live around Bojan, find that Bojan is quite interested in mixing in their culture. However, when the struggling Bojan fails to do it repeatedly, they start feeling offended by the disregard and disrespect shown by Bojan for their culture. Bojan also indulges in physical fights with the people around him, which cause chaos and disturbance in the surrounding environment.

Choi Sang-min, a minor character in *The Narrow Road to the Deep North*, is a Korean but becomes Japanese by adopting their ways of behaving and the lifestyle when the latter culture is dominant. However, later, when the rule of the Japanese is over, and all the officials of Japan are taken prisoners in Australia, he decides to assimilate with the Australian culture as the latter is dominating now. The Japanese people feel betrayed and start having trust issues with people like him. Society falls on its knees as where there are trust issues; nothing can persist. There is an acute downfall of the Japanese culture due to people like Choi Sang-min. The Doll or Ginna, the protagonist of *The Unknown Terrorist*, pretends to be associated with the dominant culture by running after the brands that the people of the dominant culture wear. She works as a promoter for the dominant culture and the people, like even the pretense of the Doll. Society gets benefitted from the wish of Doll to be like the people of that society. Mathinna, the protagonist of

Wanting, desperately wants to be like the whites, and so she tries to imitate them as much as possible by changing her choices and developing the taste as that of the elite whites. This desperation or the wish of Mathinna helps the people of the dominant culture achieve what they target. The primary purpose behind Lady Jane taking Mathinna with her in her social circle is to prove the superiority of being born in the white culture to civilize the black aboriginals. In the dominant culture, people got a toy in Mathinna to play and experiment with. However, all in all, the dominant society gets peace and scope for growth in this process of assimilation.

Another type of assimilation is pressure cooker in which the dominant society pressurizes the immigrants to get away from their culture of origin and adopt the culture of dominance. Ray, the friend of the protagonist of *First Person*, is a servant to a well-known criminal of Australia. Being from the remote areas of Tasmania, Ray is forced to be with the criminal the way the latter wants him to be. The mental state Ray is greatly affected by this pressure as he is constantly criticizing the world around him and feels homesick and suppressed all the time, and due to the pressure, he has no identity of his own. With such psyche, he affects the dominant society also in a negative way. Bojan, father of the protagonist of *The Sound of One Hand Clapping*, and the other immigrants that came in Australia with him are pressurized by the politician to forget the past and adopt the Australian lifestyle, feel homesick after a certain period but says that he "won't be allowed" to return (41, 42). He gets emotionally disturbed and craves to return to his home culture. Still, on finding that he could never do that, he develops an inferiority complex, and due to this loss of confidence and *identity crisis*, he struggles throughout his life. Similarly, in the novel *The Narrow Road to the Deep North*, the Japanese officers threaten the prisoners of war and try to tame them in the way of the Japanese lifestyle. The immigrants learn the ways but develop hatred, prejudice, and revolt against the Japanese people. This feeling causes chaos and riots against the Japanese and consequently becomes one of the reasons for the latter's downfall.

Mathinna, the protagonist of *Wanting*, is forced by Lady Jane to civilize her and make her behave the way whites behaved. The latter turns out to be very strict as she tries to lock Mathinna in a room, the windows covered with paper so that Mathinna cannot see the world outside. This mental pressure on Mathinna leads her to behave in the opposite way of her expectations. The girl starts feeling homesick and suppressed. She also feels as if she has no identity of her own. The dominant society around her also suffered along with her. The governor and his wife, Lady Jane, are embarrassed by Mathinna's savage behavior and her native dance. Apart from that, Mathinna becomes trash for society as she is useless for them and their purpose to civilize the uncivilized world.

The next process of acculturation, according to Berry's four-fold model, is segregation. It has two further sub-divisions- self-segregation or rejection and exclusive segregation. *First Person* is a complicated plot that is interwoven with the threads of different choices to opt different options in culture maintenance and rejection by the immigrant characters. The black aborigines in remote Australia choose their culture of origin over the culture of dominance. They are not lured by the baits thrown at them by the people of the dominant culture so that the former people adopt the culture of dominance. This ideology affects the people's psyche as the social effects of this cultural rejection are pretty disturbing. The black aborigines are full of hatred and vengeance for the whites, so do not let any white man enter their area and touch their women, even when they wish to marry one of the black women. This pattern causes social unrest, and all the people of majority and minority bear fatal results of the fights that germinate due to the feelings they carry for each other. The blacks start feeling alienated at some point in time and consequently land up being in depression.

Maria Magdalena Svevo, the second mother to the Aljaz in *Death of a River Guide*, is from Italy but moves to Australia for a better living. In the beginning, everything seems to work fine for her and she starts assimilating into the new culture. However, slowly she realizes the value of her own culture of origin and decides to reject the dominant culture. This transition took her from various mental tortures that she had to bear all alone. She, in the beginning, is afraid to say it openly that she lives her culture over the dominant culture, but later she becomes very open about it. She sings songs in "Triestino accent" (8) and uses the Italian phrase "Madonna Santa"

(12) again and again. Moreover, she chooses to dress up in a black dress and black hat in the style of Trieste at the funeral of Aljaz's mother rather than going with the dressing code of the dominant culture. This change in her choice of identifying only with her culture of origin gives her a new life full of hope and happiness. She succeeds in all the struggles she undergoes when she makes the wrong choice earlier. The society or the people of the dominant culture around her remain frustrated and mock her for her choice that does not fit in there. Adie, Aljaz's school friend, is "as black as him" (90), but unlike the latter, Adie is proud to be what he is. Adie seems to

have no effect on his mental state as he is too strong-minded to be affected. However, his spirit and the boldness to accept his identity openly inspire and motivate his group's people like Aljaz. He becomes a voice to the black aborigines who are constantly struggling with the *identity crisis* that they suffer from. He seems to be silently revolting against the dominant culture and the tortures given to them by the people of the dominant culture. Rose, Harry's mother, belongs to Richmond, somewhere in Europe, and marries a man of Australian origin. They move to Australia after marriage. Even after so many years of her wedding and stay in Australia among the dominant culture, she continues to love her country and her people (51). This causes difficulties in her social and marital life, but she remained firm in her choice of cultural identity. This type of acculturation affects her mental state as she feels alienated in her own house, where no one understands her. Moreover, due to her unstable and aggressive mental state, she spoils her relationship with the dominant culture people living around her. Shag, a minor character, is an Australian singer whose sister has run off to the land of the dominant culture searching for a better lifestyle and career opportunities as the latter is considered superior in all respects to the former. This incident causes unfathomable grief to Shag, who develops more and more hatred for the people of the dominant culture. This aggression is poured out through an aggressive song that he sings in the club. The society around Shag, Rose, and Maria is affected in both positive and negative ways.

The Doll, the protagonist of *The Unknown Terrorist*, tries very hard to melt into the dominant culture by pretending to be a big fan of the major brands that form a part of the people of the dominant culture. Her whole life becomes pretense, a lie, but she realizes that no matter how hard she may try to get away from her culture of origin, she cannot do that. This realization changes her life altogether. Her mental state gets disturbed as she starts getting more and more homesick each day. She faces the problem of *double consciousness* where she is not able to decide where she belongs. Due to this chaos in mind, she affects the people around her with the unpredictable behavior and abusive language she uses and addresses people with. *The Narrow Road to the Deep North* is a novel in which the Japanese rule over other countries and have taken the people of these countries as prisoners of war and have enslaved them. The condition of these immigrants is deplorable. They belong to different cultures but live together, and none of them assimilates with the dominant culture. Instead, each one of them has a different effect and different reactions to their cultural identity choice. On the one hand, Jack Rainbow, an Australian, has feelings of hatred for the Japanese and has developed an aggressive and hateful attitude towards the Japanese. On the other hand, being a hater of the people of the dominant culture, Tiny is a violent character. However, due to his strong psyche, he chooses to prove the latter inferior rather than sitting quietly or attacking the people of the majority culture. The society that comprises of the people from minority cultures as well as from the majority culture also gets affected differently. The social and psychological effects are so interrelated that these two are inseparable. The immigrants behave in a certain way with their fellow immigrants and in a certain way with the people of the majority culture. They want to show aggression to the people of the majority culture but cannot because of the latter's power, and this aggression finds its way on the fellow immigrants. This aggressive behavior disturbs the relationships of these immigrants with each other, and the suppression that took place due to the powers of the dominant people disturbs each one psychologically, causing depression, inferiority complex, lack of confidence, and even death due to inner and outer tortures.

Mathinna, the protagonist of *Wanting*, is a black aborigine who has always been fascinated by the white people of the dominant culture. When she catches the eyes of Lady Jane, she is super excited about the standard of her life that she is going to get in the dominant society. However, slowly she realizes that her native culture is very precious. From that moment on, she has a *double consciousness* as she cannot decide her cultural identity, which puts her into a mental dilemma. Despite all the efforts made by Lady Jane and her work associates, Mathinna dances her native dance in the party of the dominant class wearing a sophisticated French aristocratic dress. Her psyche disturbs all her relations with the dominant culture and the people of her tribe. The dominant society considers taming a black to be the next to impossible task and maintains the distance from the latter. Towterer, the father of Mathinna, is the leader of the aboriginal group whose members have somehow saved themselves from the people of the dominant society capturing them. Robinson and the white officials have tried their best to capture them and teach them the lifestyle and habits that the dominant society has. However, Towterer rejects to learn them and cremates the dead body of his wife according to their rituals rather than burying her the way the religion of the dominant culture teaches them. This rejection of the dominant culture makes it challenging for the people of the dominant society to achieve what they want to achieve and, as a result of that, develop more and more hatred and aggression for all the black aborigines, increasing the level of torture in their behavior for the latter. This decision to identify with their culture of origin rather than with the majority culture positively impacts the psyche of the black aborigines as they get the strength to struggle against the white dominance from their leader Towterer. However, Towterer pays for this decision personally as Robinson takes his daughter, Mathinna, to blackmail him. This incident causes much pain and mental and emotional torture to Towterer. At the societal level, this decision causes unrest, as the black aborigine people revolt openly against the dominant white society.

Bojan Buloh, the father of the protagonist of *The Sound of One Hand Clapping*, is the only character that is seen to be struggling to be identified with one culture, as in the beginning when he arrives in Australia, he rejects the culture of origin and melts down completely in the dominant culture but is unable to do it and hence tries to go back to get his identity associated with the original culture. Even by the end of the novel, he is unable to get one identity for himself. This dilemma and *double consciousness* are presented through the language and the lifestyle he uses throughout the novel. When he finally decides to segregate, he starts wearing the clothes he used to wear in his childhood and using the language that belongs to his culture of origin. This choice makes him feel positive and hopeful for a peaceful life, but this decision takes much time, which gives him psychological pressure and the feeling of *alienation*. The society around him does not affect his decision to segregate as everyone seems to be too busy to be affected. Twopenny Sal, a significant character in *Gould's Book of Fish*, is a black aborigine who somehow catches the eyes of some white men from the dominant culture. The latter wants to take her to their land, but she rejects the offer. They kidnap her son to blackmail her and promise to return her son when she comes along, which they finally succeed. However, when they reach there, they kill her son, and this incident gives her enough reason to hate the white people and take revenge on them. She lives with them, gives birth to their children as well but kills the illegitimate kids in revenge. She never accepts their lifestyle and values. This decision to segregate gives peace to her mind after she takes revenge, and the society around her start hating the black aborigines all the way more.

There is forced segregation also that takes up another form in the society and leaves a negative impact on the immigrant's mind. Boy, Aljaz's grandfather in *Death of a River Guide*, is segregated by the students from the dominant culture in school. There happens to be a birthday party of a student that belongs to the superior culture. All the class students are invited to the party except Boy because he belongs to the minority culture. This incident has a profound impact on the child's psyche, so much so that he loses confidence, starts having an inferiority complex, and suffers the after- effects of this incident throughout his life. The people of the dominant and the non- dominant cultures get affected by this incident as the people of Boy's culture and his future generations can never gain that confidence again. The people of the dominant culture get a chance to prove their superiority over the people like him.

According to J.W. Berry, the process of integration, that is maintaining relations with both the majority and the minority cultures, is subdivided as democratic pluralism, in which the choice is made by the immigrants and parental integration or inclusive segregation, in which the decision is forced by the people of the dominant culture. Both of these may have different effects on the individual and society based upon various circumstances. Aljaz, the protagonist of *Death of a River Guide*, is born in Italy but migrates to Australia with their family when he is an infant. He identifies himself with both cultures throughout his life. He dresses up in the fashion of Australia and uses some Italian phrases in his daily speech. The social relations of Aljaz seem to grow as he identifies with the people of the dominant and non-dominant cultures. The society around him seems to have no issues with him being an immigrant, and that is why there is ample scope of growth for both society and Aljaz. Tracker Marks, a minor character in *Gould's Book of Fish*, is a black man who has experience working with the American whalers and chooses to dress like them. Along with his friend Capois Death, he talks in an accent that they devise on their own. It is "a blend of English-influenced Creole and Aborigine-influenced English" (220). The existence of this process gives positive vibes to the individual as well as the people around. Society has a scope to develop as every individual who forms it is at peace. There is a birth of a language in the society that the people live.

Mr. Francis Lazaretto is a minor character in *Wanting* and belongs to Sydney. He knows Latin and Greek languages and uses them whenever he feels necessary to use them in his daily speech. He is assigned a task to teach the mannerisms and the lifestyle of the people of the dominant culture. However, in the company of Mathinna, he learns the local dance of Mathinna's tribe. Similarly, Sir John, the governor of the dominant white culture, learns the native dance and her ways from Mathinna. He finds himself at peace and enjoying her company more than with people of his own culture. On the same note, Walter Talba Bruney, Mathinna's black friend, is taught White ways and lifestyles by the protector or Robinson. He finds himself at ease with both blacks and whites. This democratic integration brings about positive well-being to Mr. Lazaretto, Walter Talba Bruney, and Sir John from inside. On the societal level, they get to make new contacts and are accessible to people from almost all over the world. They contribute to the globalization of languages and various cultures.

Fukuhara is a minor character in *The Narrow Road to the Deep North* and is Japanese and hence a part of the majority culture. People from all over the world from different cultures are taken as prisoners of war by the Japanese. Fukuhara works as a translator to Nakamura, the chief official of the Japanese army, and is also assigned a task to keep an eye on the prisoners of war. At the same time, the latter built the railway track for the Japanese government so that the Japanese could spread their culture globally by ruling the world slowly. Fukuhara knows Japanese, the dominant culture's language, and English, which is known to the rest of the world. This integration or democratic integration on the part of Fukuhara gives him a sense of superiority complex and confidence over the rest of the people in Japan. Society is also positively affected by this choice of Fukuhara as the people from the minority culture get to convey their messages to the higher officials of the dominant culture through him and vice-versa. Sonja, the protagonist of *The Sound of One Hand Clapping*, is just three years old when her father Bojan and her mother Maria bring her to Australia from Slovenia. Soon, her mother leaves her in the care of her father disappears, not to be found ever. Bojan struggles throughout his life to get one cultural identity but fails to do it as in the beginning he plans to leave his culture of origin and merge or melt in the majority culture. However, he finds himself failing at learning the language and the lifestyle of the dominant culture. Later he decides to maintain relation with hi culture of origin but again, he fails at it because of the interference of the *partial identity* that he holds of the dominant culture. However, he makes sure that his daughter learns the lifestyle of the people of the majority culture. On her sixteenth birthday, Sonja invites her friends from both cultures and prepares the food, and arranges everything suiting to the taste of all of them. This democratic integration gives mental peace and channelizes the thoughts that help her maintain her psychological well-being. Apart from the psychological level, it also affects the society around. She promotes a healthy and friendly environment by being accessible and suitable to all people from various cultures. Similarly, Moira Heaney, her friend from America who lives next door, learns Slovenian words and teaches her American accent to Sonja that remains with Sonja throughout her life. The psychological and the social effects of democratic integration are the same for Sonja, Moira Heaney and all the people sitting in the Australian club and enjoying the American songs.

Paternal integration is yet another sub-category of integration. Tracker Marks, a minor character in *Gould's Book of Fish*, is a black aborigine, who has traveled a lot with Robinson and his party, who were white, and the former learns a lot about their civilization that he liked and incorporated into his life. But he bluntly states that Robinson's party was a simple mob to travel with, but it was not his land through which he travelled, and though he was black, they were not his people. (220)

In front of the whites, Tracker Marks behaves as if he is one of them and secretly maintains his culture and ideologies, which are against those with whom and for whom he works. The nature of his work leads his dialect to be affected by it. He uses "dementung," which is a word of Van Diemonians for a dialect "that was part- blackfella, part-whitefellon." (325) He praises the white people, even though he does not like them much. The power of the majority and money in favor of the whites, makes Marks turn to their support and pretend to be like them in their presence (221). Twopenny Sal is yet another black aborigine character who always wanted to be associated with her culture of origin. However, it is forced by the people of the dominant culture to adopt their lifestyle and tastes while living among them. The Whites kidnapped the son of Twopenny Sal and blackmailed her into coming along with them, and slowly with time, due to the power and dominance of the whites, she is forced to learn the language and lifestyle which never belonged to her. This case further leads to Twopenny speaking her words for the ideologies given by the Whites. They do not mind her association with her culture of origin too. The psychological effects of this forceful integration are nasty. The individual from the minority culture, due to the pressure built by the influential people of the dominant culture, gets into a state of depression, even to the level of committing suicide. Those immigrants who are orthodox find this condition to be very challenging. There are possibilities of a state of *double consciousness* and *identity crises* as well. Society, as a result, is not found to be at peace as the orthodox people start revolting against the people of the dominant culture. However, on the positive side, it is also possible that society finds its way to develop and grow speedily.

The acculturation process has one more alternative, to choose from, for the people of a minority culture or the immigrants: marginalization. The process of marginalization has two possibilities- one, marginality, in which the decision not to follow any of the two cultures is taken by the immigrants, and two, deculturation, in which this decision is forced by the people of the dominant culture. The second possibility, according to Berry, is rare to find these days due to the education and the rules of the democratic government that promotes the right to choose for all the residents of that nation. Mathinna, the protagonist of *Wanting*, is the perfect example of the state of marginality. She tries to assimilate initially but realizes that her love for her culture of origin does not assimilate. However, her love and attraction for the dominant culture are too much to get away from it. This condition leads her to this state of marginality, where she belongs nowhere, and finally, she creates a new world for herself that is away from both cultures. She develops her ways- "neither black nor white." (213) People of her tribe stop recognizing her and call her a "black ape" (229).

Similarly, Walter Talba Bruney has rejected both cultures, and now he is confused and lost between "God, Jesus, savages, and civilization" (245). Mathinna's mental health starts deteriorating soon after she marginalizes herself. A stage comes in which "nothing matters to her" (214), and at this point, she is left alone even by her people. The Doll, the protagonist of *The Unknown Terrorist*, is a black aborigine who always tries to melt down in the dominant culture. However, when she realizes that there is no point in being associated with any of the cultures, she cuts herself off from people of both cultures. However, this affects her mental health so much so that she chooses to die in the end.

Sonja, the protagonist of *The Sound of One Hand Clapping*, integrates her native Slovenian culture and Australia's culture of dominance. However, after she conceives and is betrayed by a man, she no longer wants to be associated with any culture. There comes a time when she does not find a language to convey her message, although she knows both Slovenian and Australian. She goes through an ultimate state of depression due to *an identity crisis*. Similarly, the chaos going on in the mind of Sonja can be seen when she finds it challenging to figure out how she should address her father. Finally, she settles down halfway and addresses her father as "Dad" (37). This word is foreign to Bojan and Sonja, which belongs neither to Slovenia, the culture of origin, nor to Australia, the dominant culture. Not only Sonja but Bojan at any point in time is seen to be marginalizing him. Sonja, one day, asks her father to go home. He lies in an abyss as he belongs to nowhere. He clarifies the way he thinks about their belonging to one particular culture when he replies to Sonja's wish to return home. He says, Where? What home? You and I have no home. Don't you understand? ... We have a wog flat, my Sonja. A wog flat. Don't you understand? ...(374) The mental state of Sonja and Bojan is found to be disturbed after they decide to be cut off from both cultures. The society also gets affected by this decision as they have become very pessimistic and hopeless about everything, so the people around are not entertained or responded to with a fresh, positive attitude.

Deculturation is yet another sub-category of marginalization. This sub-category is the most negative of all, with the most harmful effects on the people's psyche and the society. Mathinna, the protagonist of *Wanting*, is a black aborigine girl who is taken to the land of the dominant white culture that she has always dreamt of. At the beginning of that new life, she tries to assimilate but fails due to her affection for the culture of origin. Later, she tries to integrate both the cultures, which is not acceptable to the people of the dominant culture, who aim to teach her their lifestyle and ways in the name of civilizing her. She is not accepted by them and is sent to an orphanage, where she still hopes to be accepted by the people of the dominant culture. However, slowly, she realizes that they do not want her to be associated with their culture, and now the people of her culture of origin do not want to accept her either. This *deculturation* causes a very negative effect on the psyche of Mathinna as she turns to the profession of prostitution and is all alone in the world. The sense of alienation and identity crisis surrounds her from all sides. Society is also very negatively affected by this. She now keeps on vomiting poison against both cultures, which is not acceptable even to her clients who abuse her a lot.

Gould, the titular character, narrator, and the protagonist of *Gould's Book of Fish*, feels "like a rat" (42) as he is rejected wherever he goes. This rejection causes a loss of confidence and gives birth to an *inferiority complex* in him. He develops an attitude of not being concerned about anyone around him, and this negative attitude spoils his relations with people of both dominant and non-dominant cultures. Similarly, Choi Sang-min, a Korean character in *The Narrow Road to the Deep North*, works in the Japanese army. However, in his schooldays in Japan, he cannot speak his mother tongue and is trained to behave like Japanese. This pressure cooker assimilation leads him nowhere because when the Japanese rule is over and the Japanese officers are being punished, he tries to tell them that he is not Japanese, but no one listens to what he says. At that point, he realizes that he belongs nowhere and has no identity of his own (322). This brings hopelessness and hollowness from inside, and he accepts the death with the wish to live no more without any identity. Jiri, a minor character in *The Sound of One Hand Clapping*, travels a lot globally. "In Czechoslovakia, he had drinks with the gypsies. In Tasmania, he drank with the aborigines. Either never accepted him, but then he, being half Sudeten German, half Czech, had never felt accepted anywhere." (114)

Jiri feels rejected everywhere as wherever he goes, the dominant culture rejects him, and till that time, he loses his own culture also. He feels that "like the Roma and the blackfellows he had never had any other choice." (115). Like Jiri, Bojan, the father of the protagonist Sonja, feels rejected and alienated as he feels that the dominant culture has never accepted him and that the people of the dominant culture also makes him leave his culture of origin leave behind by putting a condition that if he wants to grow, he needs to get rid of the past and the past culture. His daughter Sonja observes that "her father now wore clothes that spoke of nowhere, nothing, nobody, cheap clothes that were neat but shiny with wear, suggesting nothing more than a desire for comfort and warmth, of protection against the cold." (20)

Orthogonal Cultural Identification liberally allows the people to associate with two or more cultures without affecting the degree of identification with each of them. This condition is the ideal state in which there is hardly any adverse effect on society and the individual's psyche. Kif, the protagonist of *First Person,* is an aspiring author; he is hired by a company to write the biography of Australia's one of the most remarkable criminals Siegfried Heidl. The disguise of Heidl gives an impression as if he does not belong here. However, "... the beard, along with the American basketball jacket—an oddity in Australia—seemed to be about drawing attention rather than evading it." (85) Heidl and Kif have a telephonic conversation before they meet. On the phone, Kif imagines Heidl to be a person with "a soft voice" and is from Germany because of his "accent a light German." (85). Apart from the dressing style, Heidl adopts the popular terminology with the majority culture in America. There is a minor character named Frank Moretti, a pretty but disabled art collector. Frank Moretti is Italian by birth. However, good job opportunities bring him to one of the elite areas of Australia. However, his culture of origin does not affect the equal effect of the French culture on his accent. He uses both accents quite well when he speaks English. "It was as if he believed he belonged to some higher race of beings who understood Beauty and Art, who took holidays in Tuscany, and made an odd noise like the rolling of snot in the back of their throat when pronouncing Italian or French words." (128) While greeting the cops, he does this in the exact what of how Sydney people do. "It was in any case, his way with authority, his Sydney way: to smile, help, offer hospitality and friendship." (194) Dorrigo Evans, the protagonist of *The Narrow Road to the Deep North*, is an Australian, but he is fond of the Greek literature. Apart from the Greek culture, Dorrigo seems to be influenced by the American culture also. Nevertheless, the degree of his belonging to the American culture has no relation to his belonging to the Greek and Australian culture. "He drank— why would he not drink? A few whines at lunch, sometimes a whisky in his morning tea, a negroni or two before dinner (a habit he had picked from an American major while with the occupying forces in Kobe) and wine with it..." (385)

Bojan, the father of the protagonist of *The Sound of One Hand Clapping*, belongs to Slovenia and has a great love for the Slovenian traditions, values, rituals, and belief system. He loves it so much so that he maintains the degree of this identification throughout his life. However, he maintains the degrees of belongingness to other cultures also.

> "*Before drinking, Bojan gives the obligatory Slovenian toast— 'Nostrarvia!'—and they both took a few sips. 'Is it good, eh'? Bojan said. 'Apricot schnapps and leatherwood honey. Us and them. He laughed at this unlikely union of central European drink and Tasmanian food. (57)*"

Not only the degrees of these three cultures, he maintains a balance with that of Turkey also. Bojan enjoys having "Turkish coffee" (183). The psyche of Frank Moretti, Kif, Gould, Bojan and Nakamura seem to be in the ultimate ideal state as they go well with the people around, and their relations also run very smoothly. They form another level of identity that allows them to have as many cultural associations as they want. It also has very positive effects the society as a whole. The people of the society, of both dominant and non-dominant cultures, share good relations. The people realize the value of cultural competence in the growth of the society as a whole, where all the members of the society have a role to play, irrespective of their cultural identities.

The intricacies of acculturation and orthogonal cultural identification have been explored in this chapter. These two processes are very complex, as many characters associate themselves with a culture based on internal and external factors. As per their complex nature, they affect the psyche of an individual and the society very differently. In each case, various factors play their roles in shaping the fate of the characters and the people who live around them. The factors like political, economic, etc., have a significant role in deciding the effects of these processes. Effects of all the four acculturation processes given by J.W. Berry are explored along with the sub-categories of each of them. The process of assimilation has more positive than adverse effects if the choice to assimilate is made by the immigrants rather than forced. Similarly, there is a possibility of adverse effects of the integration process if the decision to integrate is forced upon the people of the minority culture by the people of the majority one. The processes of segregation and marginalization have more fatally adverse effects on the psyche of an individual and, as a result, on society as well. However, the option of orthogonal cultural identification has a rare chance of any negative impact on an individual and society.

Findings:

• Social effects

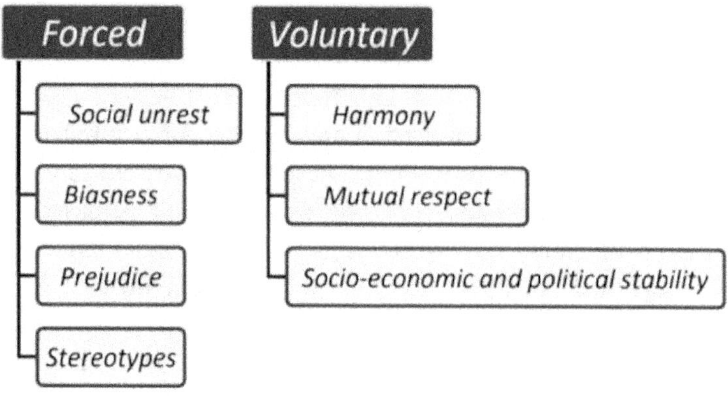

- Psychological effects

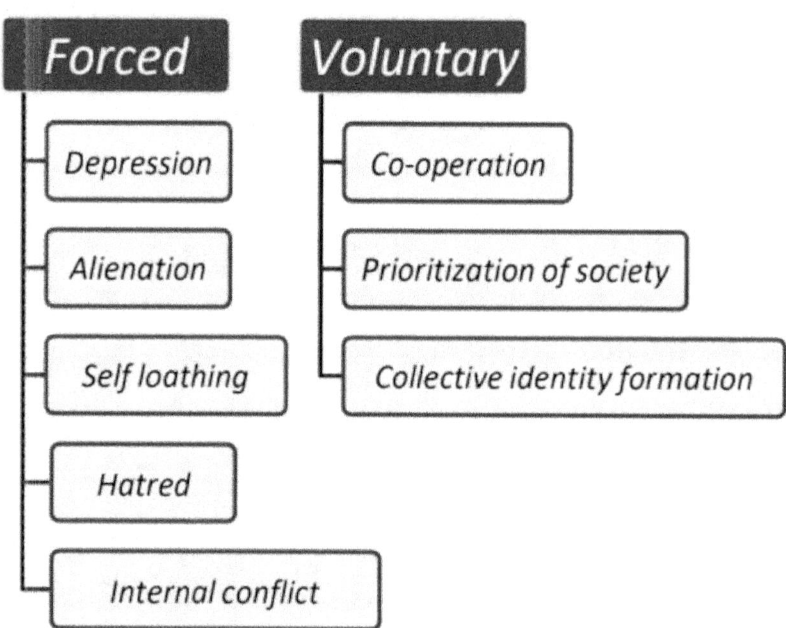

CHAPTER SIX

Conclusion

Richard Flanagan is a well-known Australian author who has bagged the Man Booker prize in 2017 for his remarkable novel *The Narrow Road to the Deep North*. He was born in Longford, Tasmania, Australia, and had Irish convict forefathers. His novels have a glimpse of his own life and significant events. Apart from weaving the storyline of his novels with various themes, he has painted his characters in blood and flesh. His characters are so lively that the reader starts relating with them immediately. He has written seven works of fiction and seven of non-fiction. In addition, he wrote four non-fiction works before he started writing fiction works, which he called "his apprenticeship." His works of fiction other than *The Narrow Road to the Deep North*, which came out in 2013, are *Death of a River Guide* in 1994, *The Sound of One Hand Clapping* in 1997, *The Unknown Terrorist* in 2006, *Gould's Book of Fish: A Book in Twelve Chapters* in 2001, *Wanting* in 2008, *First Person* in 2017.

It is said that the literature of an age is the mirror of that age. It depicts the people, lifestyle, politics, society, education, culture, values, and opinions. The present-day scenario is that there is much migration taking place from one part of the world to another; every society has become multicultural, wherein more than two cultures are co-existing, and the structure of the society and the mindset of its members and their tolerance power is rapidly changing. Therefore, the literature of this age has also taken a new shape altogether. Contemporary writers have been exploring new themes and scopes to widen the horizons to study the society and its people. Richard Flanagan has also touched upon various themes and aspects that represent those of people's lives. Culture is also one of those aspects that form a significant part of human life and hence needs an extensive study.

This study has helped us understand acculturation and its processes. Berry's four-fold model has been extensively studied and explained in chapters one, two, and three. Initially, the basic principles behind Berry's theory were understood. Later in the two subsequent chapters, the two-four processes were extensively elaborated, citing examples from Richard Flanagan's various novels. Berry's model of acculturation is based on a bi-cultural society in which one culture is dominant, and one is non-dominant. The people who belong to the non-dominant or the minority culture have to adjust to the lifestyle of the people of the dominant one. According to Berry, there are four alternatives or options in front of the migrants, out of which they follow the one that suits their needs and situation. These alternatives are based on the answer to three questions-

1. Whether the immigrant maintains his own culture or not?
2. Whether he maintains a good relationship with the host society or not?
3. Whether it is his choice to choose the answer for the first two questions or not?

With the help of a figure, Berry gave names and definitions to these four alternatives based on the answers to the questions mentioned above. The answer to the third question divides each of these four processes into two types. If the answer to the first question is 'no,' that means the immigrant does not maintain any relationship with his own culture or the culture of origin. It is a process called assimilation. Nevertheless, the answer to the third question is whether the choice of assimilating is of the individual belonging to the minority culture or forced upon him by the people of the majority one. If the decision or the choice is by the former, it is known as melting pot, and if it is forced by the latter, it is known as pressure cooker. Melting pot is a situation in which an individual or the group of individuals identifying with the minority culture willingly chooses to identify with the dominant culture and has less interest in maintaining any association with the culture of origin. However, it is the process of pressure cooker when the same circumstances occur without the wish of people of minority culture. The individual has to unwillingly forget the culture of origin and maintain relations with the majority culture.

The second process of acculturation is segregation which is also known as separation. It is a process in which, when a dominant and a non-dominant cultures come in contact, the people belonging to the minority culture reject to maintain any relationship with the majority culture and have an interest in maintaining relations with the culture of origin. Berry divided segregation based on the answer to the third question: if the people of the minority culture reject to follow the traditions, values, lifestyle, and belief system of the majority culture, it is self-segregation. Furthermore, suppose the majority culture people reject to accept the people of minority culture as part of their society and force the latter to maintain their own culture. In that case, it is what Berry terms exclusive segregation. The third acculturation process is integration which is the practical culmination of both the dominant and the non- dominant cultures. It is the most soughed one out of all the processes of acculturation. It also has two types- democratic pluralism and paternal integration. The former is the process in which the individual or a group that belongs to the non- dominant culture steps forward and maintains good relations with both the cultures, and the former is when the individual or the group of individuals maintain the relationship with both the cultures not because it is their wish, but because the people of the majority of the dominant culture want them to. Berry stated that in this type, it is not the choice of the ethnic group to carry both cultures together, and hence he gave another term to this type that is inclusive segregation. The dominant culture decides that positive relations with the dominant culture and the original ethnicity are to be maintained as it is the need of the dominant society and not the choice of the immigrants.

According to Berry, the fourth acculturation process is marginalization, which is the most negative. It has no positive outcomes and has been very rarely practiced. These days, in the times of democracy, this pattern or the process is not seen much. It is a process in which no relation is maintained with any of the cultures. According to Berry, the pattern of deculturation is very damaging as there is no hope left in the people of minority culture and suggests that the term is not appropriate as "apathy" and "withdrawal" become their "dominant feature." He suggests that although the people have their own "way of life" and how they deal with the situations, the pattern is still very "unsupportive." He terms it as a "culture of poverty." Berry, in 2006, developed a scale- "acculturation attitudes" that posed four different statements to measure which strategy out of four is most preferred and which one least. The two types of marginalization are marginality, in which the individual chooses to separate himself from his culture of origin and the dominant culture and deculturation, a process in which the individual or the group of minority culture is forced by the majority culture to remain away from the dominant culture. The latter also does not allow the former to keep any relation with their culture of origin.

The present thesis has also 'studied cultural identity and identification.' With the help of research papers and the research done till now, the scholar has tried to clear the ever-debatable difference between the two terms. Grammatically, both the terms are nouns, but there is an abstract difference between the two. The term identity means a state of self that one presents to the world, or in other words, what the world knows an individual to be, is the identity of that individual. In contrast, identification is the process of being identified as a particular individual. For instance, the scar on the leg of Odysseus proves to be a sign of his identity. It helps in the process of identification of him being Odysseus by the lady who washes the feet of this stranger and even the father of Odysseus to recognize him as his son who has been a wanderer for 20 long years. On the other hand, cultural identity is the process of being identified as a member of a particular culture, nation, ethnic group, or any group having the same characteristics. There has been much debate as most people use the terms 'Cultural identity and 'ethnic identity interchangeably. However, the fact is that both these terms differ in meaning. On the one hand, cultural identity is when people of a group or an individual have a sense of belongingness to a particular culture. In contrast, ethnic identity is a sense of belongingness that relates a group of people to another group or an individual to another. Thus, cultural identity is an umbrella term that includes a social and ethnic identity.

The present thesis has explored the intricacies of acculturation and orthogonal cultural identification. With the help of textual analysis of the novels of Richard Flanagan, the psychological and social complexities created by these two are explored. When two cultures interact or try to co-exist, the lives of the individuals belonging to both the dominant and the non-dominant cultures are affected. Mostly the people of a minority culture are affected by this interaction. Berry's four-fold model of acculturation has been taken as the standard measure, as it covers all the categories and sub-categories of people and the various types of processes that may occur during cultural interaction. Each of the four processes and further each type of these processes has a different impact on the psyche of an individual and the society as a whole. Similarly, orthogonal cultural identification has many psychological and social complications as an after effect.

The process of assimilation colors life and the atmosphere of society with complementary colors if the decision of melting in the larger society is taken by the individual from his own will. For instance, Bojan, the father of the protagonist of *The Sound of One Hand Clapping*, his daughter Sonja, the protagonist, Choi Sang-min, a minor character in *The Narrow Road to the Deep North*, Ginna or the Doll, the protagonist of *The Unknown Terrorist*, Mathinna, the protagonist of *Wanting*, Maria Magdalena Svevo, one of the central characters of *The Death of a River Guide*, and Aljaz, the protagonist of *The Death of a River Guide*, all meld down in the majority culture with their wish and will and hence, initially, the lives of all of them is very peaceful. However, over time, the culture of origin that they tend to leave behind starts intervening. After some time of assimilating, some characters show the sign of missing the culture of origin, feeling depressed and homesick. The characters in this category are Bojan, Mathinna, Maria Magdalena Svevo, and Choi Sang-min. The characters in this category are Aljaz, Sonja, and Ginna, who seem very happy throughout. After some time of assimilating, the characters who face challenges try to follow other alternating processes as per their situations.

The second sub-category of assimilation is a forced one, that is pressure cooker, and in this category the problems are opposite to the previous one. Flanagan's all novels have one or the other characters representing this part of the society that is forced to assimilate in the majority culture and leave the culture behind. Twopenny Sal, a character in *Gould's Book of Fish*, Bojan, the father of the protagonist of *The Sound of One Hand Clapping*, the POWs in *The Narrow Road to the Deep North*, Towterer, the father of the protagonist of *Wanting* and Mathinna, the protagonist of *Wanting* are a few examples of this category. The problem with the forced assimilation is that the people who are forced develop a sort of rebellion inside them, but some of them, who cannot revolt and are not strong enough to participate in the riots, develop one or the other psychological issues and suffer internally rather than expressing externally. The characters which suffer due to the choices made by themselves are Bojan and Mathinna, who blame themselves for not being able to assimilate as desired by the majority culture's people. Nevertheless, there are some characters like Towterer, who is forced by emotional blackmailing in the name of his daughter Mathinna, who makes a group of people like him and attack the people of majority culture whenever they get a chance. However, there are people like Twopenny Sal also who take revenge later and do not openly revolt. For example, the people of the majority culture force Twopenny Sal to be their slaves and move to their land by blackmailing her in the name of her son, but later, the moment she lands in the latter's country, they still kill her son.

However, later on, she takes revenge by killing the children she gives birth with her masters.

The process of segregation impacts an individual or a group of individuals who belong to the minority culture in both negative and positive ways. For example, suppose the people of majority culture reject the people of the minority culture and want them to stick to the traditions and the values of their culture of origin. In that case, it is called exclusive segregation, and it has harmful colors to color the lives of the people of minority culture. It affects the psychology of the individuals a lot, making them feel depressed and giving birth to feelings like aggression and violence. The characters from the novels of Richard Flanagan very well represent the effects of exclusive segregation. The characters like Bojan and all the people who migrated with him to Australia are treated so that they are made to feel that they do not belong to that place. Their houses are separate, and they are called wog houses to segregate them from the mainstream. Bojan and the rest of the immigrants feel depressed, and they express how much they are affected in their conversations with each other. Aljaz, the protagonist of *Death of a River* Guide, suffers the same situation in school that he carries throughout his life and feels terrible and depressed about how the children of his school left him for every birthday party they joined together.

Moreover, even the teachers of his school mistreat him just because he is an immigrant and not one of those who belonged to the majority culture. Then another category of characters revolt after being forced to segregate like the POWs in Japan in *The Narrow Road to the Deep North*. These characters are shown to be suppressed a0nd forced not to adopt the Japanese culture, so much so that later when the circumstances turn in favor of the people who once used to be prisoners, the latter take revenge by forming groups and forcing the formers to leave their own country and run.

Segregation has a positive sub-category also and that is 'self-rejection.' Characters like Rolo Palma, a minor character in *The Unknown Terrorist*, Twopenny Sal, an essential character in *Gould's Book of Fish*, Bojan, the father of the protagonist of *The Sound of One Hand Clapping* and Maria, the mother of the protagonist of the same novel, Towterer, the father of the protagonist of *Wanting* and Nakamura, a central Japanese character in *The Narrow Road to the Deep North*, fall under this category. These characters initially feel everything to be all right, but later on, they find this process very isolating as they cannot mix with the people around them due to their orthodox thought process. The following process by Berry is Integration, which is the most positive of all four. The problem with democratic integration or democratic pluralism is that the degree of identification or association with more than one culture cannot be measured and kept in mind. Otherwise, this process of integration has no negative implications, neither on an individual's life nor on society as a whole. The characters in the novels of Richard Flanagan very well portray this sub-category of integration and seem to be entirely happy and progressing. Mathinna and Mr. Francis Lazaretto from *Wanting* and Sonja Buloh and Bojan Buloh from the novel *The Sound of One Hand Clapping* fall under this category. In a few cases, a new language is born, typically by the mixture of the dominant and the non-dominant cultures. Parental Integration is the second sub- category of the process of integration. Although this process is by the demand of the majority people and is forced upon the people of the minority culture, there are not many issues initially. Later on, the characters of the novels of Richard Flanagan portray some signs of aggression and rebellious attitude later in their lives, after the chains of their culture of origin start intervening and stopping them from doing what is expected by the people of the dominant culture. Tracker Marks, for instance, from *Gould's Book of Fish*, is the best example of parental integration. He starts pretending to be following the dominant culture sometime later, which further leads to hatred and frustration in his heart later on.

The fourth process named by J.W. Berry is marginalization. It is a process in which the people of minority culture do not belong to any one culture, neither the dominant one nor the non-dominant one. It has two types- marginality and deculturation where both the sub-categories have their problems, and different characters of the novels of Richard Flanagan react to each one of them differently, based on the situation they are in. The problem with marginality is that although the process is chosen by the individual on his own, without any external or internal pressure, at some point of time, there are possibilities of facing the issue of alienation, loss of identity, and depression because they will not be able to participate in the events going on around them. The characters of Flanagan's fiction very well present the psychological and social conditions and their effects. Mathinna, the protagonist of *Wanting*, towards the end, shows the signs of self withdrawal from both cultures and jumps into the profession of prostitution when she realizes that there is no other option left for her. Not only Mathinna but other characters like Choi Sang-min, a minor character in *The Narrow Road to the Deep North*, Doll or Ginna, the protagonist of *The Unknown Terrorist*, Bojan from *The Sound of One Hand Clapping* also show similar signs of marginality. The problem arises later in the lives of the characters when the society they live in starts bothering them in their daily lifestyle. The characters feel the lonely and alienated atmosphere they have created on their own, and then some of them feel depressed like Bojan and Choi Sang-min, and a few commit suicide or their lives become vulnerable at the end, like the Doll and Mathinna. One more type of marginalization is more disastrous than marginality and that is deculturation. The difference between the two is that the latter is forced upon the minority culture by the people of the majority culture. The problem with this type of marginalization is that there are chances of revolts and violence from the people of minority culture on the societal level and loss of identity, depression, and alienation on the individual level. For instance, the blacks in the novel *Death of a River Guide* are not allowed to leave their culture or adopt the dominant culture. They hence are left on the island to have a life with no cultural identity and give birth to the children of free white settlers and the convicts. Similarly, the characters like Choi Sang-min from *The Narrow Road to the Deep North*, Mr. Lempriere, a minor character in *Gould's Book of Fish*, Robinson or the Protector in *Wanting,* and Bojan and Jiri in *The Sound of One Hand Clapping* are forced to lose their identity as the people in power or the people of the dominant culture do not allow them to follow any culture. There is a possibility of revolt in this case of marginalization, but the characters of Richard Flanagan do not show any sign of violence.

The present study also traced the orthogonal cultural identification in the works of Richard Flanagan. Orthogonal Cultural Identification is a liberal approach that allows the minority culture to adopt any number of cultures they want to adopt. Unlike other acculturation theories, it talks about the people of the majority culture as well. It considers that the degree of identification with one culture may differ from the degree of identification with other cultures and that these degrees do not affect each other. There are many characters in the fiction of Richard Flanagan who opt for the option of adopting more than two cultures at a time. Kif and Heidl from *The First Person*, Frank Moretti from *The Unknown Terrorist*, Dorrigo, Rooster MacNeice and The wife of Old Jackie from *The Narrow Road to the Deep North*, Bojan, Sonja, Jiri, and the minor character Moira Heaney from *The Sound of One Hand Clapping*, William Gould, the protagonist of

Gould's Book of Fish, and Twopenny Sal from the same novel, Aljaz Cosini, Lou, Maria Magdalena Svevo and Aunt Ellie in *Death of a River Guide* and Mathinna, Mr. Francis Lazaretto and the governor Mr. John in *Wanting* are the ones who adopt more than one culture at a time and do not let the degree of association with other cultures affect the degree of belongingness top another culture. Some of these characters adopt the language of other cultures, while some choose the aspects of lifestyle. Dorrigo considers intercultural relations and connections to be perfectly all right. He has read about the culture, values, traditions, and belief systems of the Greeks. He has also adopted some of them without affecting the degree of belongingness to his own Australian culture. Apart from the Greek culture, Dorrigo seems to be influenced by the American culture also. However, here again, the degree of his belonging to the American culture has no relation to his belonging to the Greek and Australian culture. Bojan, for instance, belongs to Slovenia and has a great love for the Slovenian traditions, values, rituals, and belief systems. He loves it so much so that he maintains the degree of this identification throughout his life. However, he maintains the degrees of his belongingness to other cultures also. Not only the degrees of these three cultures, he maintains a balance with that of Turkey also.

The theories of acculturation and orthogonal cultural identification have been applied to the works of Richard Flanagan. There are various theories in acculturation given by distinguished scholars. However, many eminent scholars consider J.W. Berry's four-fold model to be the best. It is thought to have covered all the possibilities of two cultures coming together and trying to co-exist. The only issue that has been observed by the scholars in the model is that it discusses the people of minority culture and has no mention about the people of majority culture as if only the former is affected by the process and has a notion that it is only the people who belong to the culture of the minority have to change, suffer and adapt. However, the life of the people of the majority culture remains as it is. Nevertheless, the theory of orthogonal cultural identification fills in the gap left by the best theory of acculturation. The characters of Flanagan's novels represent all the categories and sub-categories of acculturation and orthogonal cultural identification and very well present the intricacies of the complexities created by the occurrence of these two processes in the society at two levels- individual level, covering the psychological and behavioral changes that occur within and societal level, covering the changes that occur in the values and belief system of the more significant and the smaller society.

Bojan, the father of the protagonist of *The Sound of One Hand Clapping*, and Mathinna, the protagonist of *Wanting*, are the only two characters through all the seven novels who go through all the four processes of acculturation, giving a better insight into the effects of all four of them at both individuals as well as societal level. These two characters present a more realistic picture of the actual people in contemporary society as they face many challenges and keep changing their cultural orientation as and when needed. Bojan is seen struggling throughout the novel, and similarly, Mathinna also suffers and fights with her mind and, in the end, lands up being a prostitute because of the loss of cultural identity after all the struggle.

After analyzing the texts and studying the changes that took place in the individual and the society as a whole due to the processes of acculturation and orthogonal cultural identification, it has been observed that all the processes of acculturation have one or the other issues due to which the characters suffer a lot. As the characters represent the real people of contemporary society and they suffer the outcomes of the processes, the people will also suffer in the process of amalgamation of two or more cultures. The effective solution brought out through the study of the novels, is that the process of democratic pluralism is best by keeping in mind that the degree of identification with one culture is not related to the degree of identification to another culture or cultures. The increase or decrease in the degree of identification with one culture can never affect the increase or decrease in the degree of identification with other cultures or cultures.

The present study has also explored the social and psychological intricacies of acculturation and orthogonal cultural identification. It has focused on Richard Flanagan's fiction as the fictional characters represent the people of contemporary society. It is considered that this study applies to the real society and the actual immigrants as well. The study was limited because of its objective-oriented nature, but there is much scope for future studies, which this study cannot cover. In the future, the research can be done on the case studies or real-life experiences of the actual immigrants of various cultures. Other aspects of the effects of these two approaches, like political, economic, health-related, religious, and geographic, can also be studied.The changing trends and the socio-political changes have given birth to a new type of acculturation that is 'globalization based acculturation' which leads toharmony in the society.

Factors like age, gender, sex, educational level etc affect the cultural orientation of individual as well as a group. These factors can be cushioned through media and state policies, providing adequate space to every individual. These models prove that the monolithic nature of the cultural orientation is notpossible and also suggest the effective ways of achieving plurality. Orthogonal Cultural Identification widens the scope and horizon of different cultures as it gives liberty to an individual to have different degrees of identification with more than two cultures. The dominant culture is propagated and the non-dominant culture is stifled by the policies of the state, language of the judicial statements and also the language used during the process of cultural interaction. Cultural interaction is woven with the threads of ambiguity and contradictions. This can be tackled by providing a linear socio-cultural environment by foregrounding Orthogonal Cultural Identification.

Bibliography

Primary Sources-

Flanagan, Richard. *Death of a River Guide*. Penguin, 1994.

---, *First Person*. Penguin, 2017.

---, Gould's Book of Fish: A Novel in Twelve Fish. Penguin, 2001.

---, *The Narrow Road to the Deep North*. Penguin, 2013.

---, *The Sound of One Hand Clapping*. Penguin, 1997.

---, *The Unknown Terrorist*. Penguin, 2006.

---, *Wanting*. Penguin, 2008.

Secondary Sources-

"Lecture 11- Acculturation, Assimilation and Integration." *YouTube*, uploaded by NIOSSeniorSecondaryCourses, 24 October 2018, https://www.youtube.com/watch?v=6oJIvAG1qKs.

Alphonse, Mary, Purnima George, and Ken Moffatt. "Redefining social work standards in the context of globalization: Lessons from India." *International Social Work* 51.2 (2008): 145-158.

Anderson, Shannon Latkin. *Immigration, assimilation, and the cultural construction of American national identity*. Routledge, 2015.

Antor, Heinz. "The Trauma of Immigration and the Ethics of Self-Positioning in Richard Flanagan's The Sound of One Hand Clapping." *The Splintered Glass*. Brill Rodopi, 2011. 205-220.

Arimitsu, Yasue. "Richard Flanagan's The Narrow Road to the Deep North and Matsuo Basho's Oku no Hosomichi." *Coolabah* 21 (2017): 6-23.

Ausubel, David P. "Acculturative stress in modern Maori adolescence." *Child Development* (1960): 617-631.

Basho, Matsuo. *The narrow road to the deep north and other travel sketches*. Penguin UK, 2020.

Ben-Messahel, Salhia. "Colonial desire and the renaming of history in Richard Flanagan's' Wanting'." *Commonwealth Essays and Studies* 36.1 (2013): 21-32.

Berry, J. W. "Marginality, Stress and IdentiJication in An Acculturating Aboriginal Communify." *Journal of Cross-Cultural Psychology* (1970): 1-239.

--, "A psychology of immigration." *Journal of social issues* 57.3 (2001): 615-631.

---, "Acculturation and adaptation in a new society." International migration 30 (992): 69-69.

---, "Acculturation and health." *Cultural clinical psychology: Theory, research, and practice* (1998): 39-57.

---, "Acculturation and adaptation in a new society." *International migration* 30 (1992): 69-69.

---, "Immigration, acculturation, and adaptation." *Applied psychology* 46.1 (1997): 5- 34.

---, "Integration and multiculturalism: Ways towards social solidarity." *Papers on social representations* 20.1 (2011): 2-1.

---, "Psychological aspects of cultural pluralism." Cultural Learning, 2, 17-22.

---, "Psychological aspects of cultural pluralism: unity and identity reconsidered." Topics in culture learning 2 (1974): 17-22.

---, "Stress perspectives on acculturation." (2006).

Berry, John W., et al. "Acculturation attitudes in plural societies." *Applied psychology* 38.2 (1989): 185-206.

Boski, Pawel, Katarzyna Strus, and Ewa Tlaga. "Cultural identity, existential anxiety and traditionalism." (2004).

Caravantes, Ernesto. *From Melting Pot to Witch's Cauldron: How Multiculturalism Failed America.* Government Institutes, 2010.

Dinnerstein, Leonard. *Ethnic Americans: A history of immigration.* Columbia University Press, 2009.

Foster, Janet. "Social exclusion, crime and drugs." *Drugs: education, prevention and policy* 7.4 (2000): 317-330.

Fredrickson, George M. "Models of American ethnic relations: A historical perspective." (1999).

Grundlingh, Georgia. "Inventing the Past: Regional Myth in Michael Crummey's Galore and Richard Flanagan's Gould's Book of Fish." (2014).

Hirsch, Walter. "Assimilation as Concept and as Process." Social Forces (1942): 35- 39.

Ishak, Noriza, Mohd Salehuddin Mohd Zahari, and Zulhan Othman. "Influence of acculturation on foodways among ethnic groups and common acceptable food." *Procedia-Social and Behavioral Sciences* 105 (2013): 438-444.

Jackson II, Ronald L., and Michael A. Hogg, eds. *Encyclopedia of identity.* Vol. 1. Sage, 2010.

Jensen, Lars. "The Narrow Road to the Deep North and the De-sacralisation of the Nation." *Le Simplegadi* 16 (2016): 74-85.

Jones, Joanne. "History and the Novel: Refusing to be Silent." *Westerly* 55.2 (2010): 36-52.

Kagitcibasi, Cigdem. "Autonomy and relatedness in cultural context: Implications for self and family." *Journal of cross-cultural psychology* 36.4 (2005): 403-422.

Karim, Karim H. "Nation and diaspora: Rethinking multiculturalism in a transnational context." *International Journal of Media & Cultural Politics* 2.3 (2007): 267-282.

Kramer, Eric Mark. "Cultural fusion and the defense of difference." *Socio-cultural conflict between African and Korean Americans* (2000): 182-223.

Kwak, K., B. Ataca, and J. W. Berry. "Canada family bonds among Canadian university students." International Journal of Psychology. Vol. 35. No. 3-4. 27 Church RD, Hove BN3 2FA, East Sussex, England: Psychology Press, 2000.

Lai-Ming, Tammy Ho. "Cannibalised Girlhood in Richard Flanagan's Wanting." *Neo-Victorian Studies* 5.1 (2012): 14-37.

Lower, Timothy A. *The Orthogonal Cultural Identification Scale in Asian Indian International Exchange Students: A Qualitative Study of Meanings Ascribed to Scale Items*. Diss. 2008.

Lueck, Kerstin, and Machelle Wilson. "Acculturative stress in Latino immigrants: The impact of social, socio-psychological and migration-related factors." *International Journal of Intercultural Relations* 35.2 (2011): 186-195.

Lustig, Myron W., Jolene Koester, and Rona Halualani. *Intercultural competence: Interpersonal communication across cultures*. Pearson/A and B, 2006.

Maji, Pew. "Representation of War in Richard Flanagan's The Narrow Road to the Deep North." *The Criterion* 8.1 (2017): 953-957.

Marginalisation. *The Free Dictionary*, http://www.thefreedictionary.com/marginalisation. Accessed 19 May 2021.

Markosová, Bianka. *Living Conditions in Van Diemen's Land in Clarke's For the Term of His Natural Life and Flanagan's Gould's Book of Fish*. 2009. Masarykova University, PhD dissertation.

MENEK, İbrahim Halil. "A HISTORICAL EXAMPLE OF MULTICULTURALISM: ACHAEMENID EMPIRE MULTICULTURALISM." *Gaziantep Üniversitesi İktisadi ve İdari Bilimler Fakültesi Dergisi* 2.1: 118-138.

Musleh, Tarek. "Political Power in Narrow Road to the Deep North: Between Asian Tyranny and Western Imperialism."

Nash, Kate. "Introduction to sociology." *Introducing the Social Sciences for Midwifery Practice*. Routledge, 2015. 1-19.

Ng Tseung-Wong, Caroline, and Maykel Verkuyten. "Multiculturalism, Mauritian style: Cultural diversity, belonging, and a secular state." *American Behavioral Scientist* 59.6 (2015): 679-701.

Ng, Eddy S., and Irene Bloemraad. "A SWOT analysis of multiculturalism in Canada, Europe, Mauritius, and South Korea." (2015): 619-636.

Ngo, Van Hieu. *A critical examination of acculturation theories*. Critical social work 9.1 (2008): 1-6.

Nguyen, Angela- MinhTu D., and Verónica Benet- Martínez. "Biculturalism unpacked: Components, measurement, individual differences, and outcomes." *Social and Personality Psychology Compass* 1.1 (2007): 101-114.

Oetting, Eugene R., and Fred Beauvais. "Orthogonal cultural identification theory: The cultural identification of minority adolescents." *International journal of the addictions* 25.sup5 (1991): 655-685.

Oetting, Eugene R., et al. "Primary socialization theory: Culture, ethnicity, and cultural identification. The links between culture and substance use. IV." *Substance Use & Misuse* 33.10 (1998): 2075-2107.

Oetting, Eugene R., Randall C. Swaim, and Maria Carla Chiarella. "Factor structure and invariance of the orthogonal cultural identification scale among American Indian and Mexican American youth." *Hispanic Journal of Behavioral Sciences* 20.2 (1998): 131-154.

Orbe, Mark P. "African American communication research: Toward a deeper understanding of interethnic communication." *Western Journal of Communication (includes Communication Reports)* 59.1 (1995): 61-78.

---, "From the standpoint (s) of traditionally muted groups: Explicating a co-cultural communication theoretical model." *Communication Theory* 8.1 (1998): 1-26.

---, *Constructing co-cultural theory: An explication of culture, power, and communication*. Sage Publications, 1997.

Orthogonal Theory. *Iresearchnet.com*, http://psychology.iresearchnet.com/counseling-psychology/counseling-theories/orthogonal-theory/. Accessed 25 April 2021.

Parekh, Bhikhu. "Rethinking multiculturalism: Cultural diversity and political theory." *Ethnicities* 1.1 (2001): 109-115.

Park, Robert Ezra, and Ernest Watson Burgess. Introduction to the Science of Sociology. Good Press, 2019.

Parsons, Elsie Clews. "Mitla, Town of Souls. University of Chicago Publications in Anthropology." (1936).

Piontkowski, Ursula, et al. "Predicting acculturation attitudes of dominant and non- dominant groups." International Journal of Intercultural Relations 24.1 (2000): 1-26.

Polack, Fiona Margaret. *Littoral fictions: Writing Tasmania and Newfoundland*. 2002. University of Tasmania, PhD dissertation.

Reed, Sarah Margaret Anne. *The perils of translation: the representation of Australian cultural identity in the French translations of crime fiction novels by Richard Flanagan and Philip McLaren*. 2015. University of Adelaide, PhD dissertation.

Rudmin, Floyd W. "Critical history of the acculturation psychology of assimilation, separation, integration, and marginalization." *Review of general psychology* 7.1 (2003): 3-37.

Sam, David L., and John W. Berry. "Acculturation: When individuals and groups of different cultural backgrounds meet." *Perspectives on psychological science* 5.4 (2010): 472-481.

Sanchez-Burks, J., R. E. Nisbett, and O. Ybarra. "Cultural Styles, Relational Schemas and Prejudice Against Outgroups. 2000." *University of Michigan*.

Saroha, Rashmi. "Acculturation Strategies." Youtube, 16 Oct. 2016, https://www.youtube.com/watch?v=vQxs6IsFbtM.

Schumpeter, Joseph A. *History of economic analysis*. Routledge, 2006.

Schwartz, Seth J., et al. "Rethinking the concept of acculturation: implications for theory and research." *American Psychologist* 65.4 (2010): 237.

Seddon, Toby. "Drugs, crime and social exclusion: social context and social theory in British drugs–crime research." *British Journal of Criminology* 46.4 (2006): 680-703.

Sharma, Rahul. "Marginalization." YouTube, 18 June 2018, https://www.youtube.com/watch?v=7V5kmanmM0g.

Silva, Nicole Da, et al. "Acculturative stress, psychological distress, and religious coping among Latina young adult immigrants." *The Counseling Psychologist* 45.2 (2017): 213-236

Skilton, St John. "Book review: CW WATSON, Multiculturalism. Buckingham: Open University Press, 2000. 124 pp. ISBN 0 335 2052 0." *Discourse Studies* 4.2 (2002): 259-261.

Staff. "Pluralism, Cultural." *Encyclopedia of Special Education* (2008): 1591-1592.

Staniforth, Martin. ""Shades of the prison house": Reading Richard Flanagan's The Narrow Road to the Deep North and Peter Carey's Amnesia." *Journal of Postcolonial Writing* 53.5 (2017): 578-589.

Staniforth, Martin. ""Shades of the prison house": Reading Richard Flanagan's The Narrow Road to the Deep North and Peter Carey's Amnesia." *Journal of Postcolonial Writing* 53.5 (2017): 578-589.

Stigler, George. "The adoption of the marginal utility theory." *Quarterly Journal of Business and Economics* 11.4 (1972): 188.

Strehle, Susan. "War and Communities of Suffering: Richard Flanagan, The Narrow Road to the Deep North." *Contemporary Historical Fiction, Exceptionalism and Community*. Palgrave Macmillan, Cham, 2020. 77-102.

Tedlock, Dennis, and Bruce Mannheim, eds. *The dialogic emergence of culture.*University of Illinois Press, 1995.

Todd, Loreto. *Pidgins and creoles*. Routledge, 2003.

Toomey, Stella Ting. Wiley Online Library, 13 December 2017, https://onlinelibrary.wiley.com/doi/abs/10.1002/9781118783665.ieicc0039 Accessed 27 May 2021.

Vrooman, J. Cok, and Stella JM Hoff. "The disadvantaged among the Dutch: A survey approach to the multidimensional measurement of social exclusion." *Social indicators research* 113.3 (2013): 1261-1287.

Wallhead Salway, Celia Margaret. "To voice or not to voice the Tasmanian Aborigines: novels by Matthew Kneale and Richard Flanagan." *Revista alicantina de estudios ingleses, No. 16, 2003, pp. 283-295.*

Wang, Yikang, et al. "Cross-cultural adaptation of international college students in the United States." *Journal of international students* 8.2 (2018): 821-842.

Watts, Richard J., and Jerzy Jaroslaw Smolicz. *Cultural democracy and ethnic pluralism: Multicultural and multilingual policies in education*. Peter Lang, 1997.

Werbner, Richard. *The Politics of Multiculturalism in the New Europe: Racism, Identity and Community*. Palgrave Macmillan, 1997.

What is Cultural Identity. *IGI Global*, https://www.igi-global.com/dictionary/cultural-self-study-as-a-tool-for-critical-reflection-

and-learning/6396. Accessed 13 July 2021.

White, Laura A. "Submerging the imperial eye: Affective narration as environmentalist intervention in Richard Flanagan's Death of a River Guide." *The Journal of Commonwealth Literature* 47.2 (2012): 265-279.

Wickström, Mats. "The multicultural moment: the history of the idea and politics of multiculturalism in Sweden in comparative, transnational and biographical context." (2015): 1964–1975.

Zhou, Min. "Segmented assimilation: Issues, controversies, and recent research on the new second generation." *International migration review* 31.4 (1997): 975- 1008.